MW01234277

SPAZ

The True Story
of My Life
with ADHD

Leigh Macneil **with** Renee Macneil

authorHOUSE®

AuthorHouse™
1663 Liberty Drive
Bloomington, IN 47403
www.authorhouse.com
Phone: 1 (800) 839-8640

We have tried to recreate events, locales and conversations from my memories of them.
In order to maintain their anonymity in some instances we have changed the names
of individuals and places, We may have changed some identifying characteristics
and details such as physical properties, occupations and places of residence.

Published by AuthorHouse 09/20/2017

ISBN: 978-1-5462-0930-0 (sc)
ISBN: 978-1-5462-0929-4 (e)

Library of Congress Control Number: 2017914457

Print information available on the last page.

Any people depicted in stock imagery provided by Thinkstock are models,
and such images are being used for illustrative purposes only.
Certain stock imagery © Thinkstock.

This book is printed on acid-free paper.

CONTENTS

Conversation between father and daughter:

"Daddy, you have ADHD just like me, right?"

"That's right."

"Is that bad ?"

"No, honey, it's not bad."

"But what does it mean?"

"It means that the rest of the world moves too slowly for us."

PREFACE

I have always told the stories of my childhood as if they were a punchline to the joke that is my ADHD. I used them to further my label as a class clown. I told them to entertain people and to poke fun at myself. At least, that is why I thought I told them. Deep down, though, I knew a different truth. I told them to cover up years of pain and embarrassment. I thought if I made fun of myself, then no one else would be able to make fun of me. I was afraid to let people know how hard I had struggled to get where I am. I was scared that my vulnerability would show my weaknesses. I did not want to be Spaz anymore. I was shocked when one of my wife's friends told her that she felt inspired by my life stories. She told Renee that my tales gave her hope for a decent future for her young son who struggles with severe ADHD. This concept planted a seed that would take several years to grow. Now, a tree in full bloom, this book has emerged. It is my deepest desire that others, whether they are people with ADHD, relatives of people with ADHD, educators, doctors, friends, or simply avid readers who want a good story, will be inspired by these stories as well.

This book exists because I managed to overcome adversities in my life—complications that stemmed from my ADHD. Despite the many obstacles I faced, I came out with a successful career and a wonderful family. The path to this happy ending was not smooth, nor was it pleasant. I felt very alone throughout my life. It is my hope that this book will help others realize that they never have to feel that isolated. When you are surrounded by negative talk, especially when it comes from those closest to you, it can be easy for you to start to believe it. You withdraw from others simply due to your own insecurities and your depreciation of your own self-worth while others separate themselves from you because you are, a "troublemaker," a "weirdo," the "hyper-guy," "quick-to-anger," a "Spaz." Suddenly you look around and no one has your back. Not even you.

I have been there. Sometimes I still feel like I am there, but I have had to learn how to prevail. While my emotional pain and struggle may not be visible to the eye, they are what has motivated me and propelled me into every success story that I have. I want to show the world that, even when the odds seem to be stacked against you, you do not have to cater to the odds. In fact, if you're a little bit "different", like me, then you shouldn't follow the odds because they apply to the average, "normal", person and that's simply not us.

Even though I have embraced my ADHD, I dislike the name Attention Deficit Hyperactive Disorder. Disorder sounds so ugly. It implies that there is some glitch or error in my body and I refuse to look at myself that way. I tell people that I don't have ADHD; I have ADHA, Attention Deficit Hyperactive *Advantage*. Many of the quirks of my ADHD are the very things that have helped me achieve various accomplishments in my life. I did not always feel this way, however. Most of my youth was spent in layers of sadness, frustration, depression, and confusion. It was not until I entered adulthood that I truly began to understand how my brain worked and how I could use the things I once thought to be my shortcomings to my advantage.

Throughout this book, you will learn about some of the science behind the behaviors associated with ADHD. Much of that science, despite being "proven" is still being researched and debated. My wife, Renee, and I have structured this book in a unique way. We alternated my real-life stories with informational text full of suggestions based on statistics, research, Renee's background in education, and her knowledge of ADHD and ADHD coaching. Some of this information is subjective and stems from our own beliefs, ideas, and experiences. Other information is based on the work of ADHD experts and is denoted as such. These expository pieces are designed to shed light on the characteristics and traits of ADHD that are at work in the story that immediately follows. While some of these introductory pieces might contain disheartening information, I urge you to realize that you are not defined by someone else's definition of Attention Deficit Hyperactive Disorder. Regardless of your "disability", you have special gifts that make you great.

Only you can bring out those special gifts through the actions you take. For most of my life I was told that my disability would keep me from doing the things that I wanted to do. I suffered through a lot of internal pain because of that. However, I found ways to unearth the strength within myself and to keep moving forward towards my goals. It is my hope that this book will inspire others to do the same. Whether you are someone with ADHD or you know someone with ADHD, Renee and I believe that this book will give you the insight, understanding, and inspiration to follow your own dreams.

Today there are many resources available to help you understand ADHD. Renee and I hope that you look at this book as a great starting point. But, if it does nothing more than make you smile, I will still count it as the success of a former class clown. This tiny seed that has flourished and flowered is my story. Who am I?

I am Spaz.

CHAPTER ONE

PASS THE BUCK

When my wife discusses the developmental delay caused by ADHD with anyone, regardless of if they thought they knew it all already, they are always totally and utterly blown away. The science now shows that, although the brain of an ADHDer seems to mature in a normal way, there are elements of it that are delayed for an average of about three years. This developmental delay generally affects the cortex, or the part of the brain associated with executive function. A study using brain scans at the National Institute of Health confirmed the delay in the thickening of the pre-frontal cortex in children with ADHD. "These frontal areas support the ability to suppress inappropriate actions and thoughts, focus attention, remember things from moment to moment, work for reward, and control movement" ("Brain...," 2007). These are the very things affected by Attention Deficit Hyperactive Disorder. This means that a child with ADHD operates three years behind the average child in these functions.

Along with a struggle in executive functions comes an apparent emotional immaturity. Therefore, a child who is biologically eight years old may have the emotional maturity of a five-year-old. A child who is eighteen may only be able to function at the same level as a much younger teenager. This is shocking for parents to hear, but it is also enlightening and can be a bit of a relief. There is some freedom in realizing that the reason your six-year-old can't get his shoes on to get out the door in time for school is because he's actually functioning at the emotional maturity level of a three, or four-year-old. Tying shoes is not high on a three-year-old's priority list, nor is it always physically possible for someone who is operating at that age level.

Additionally, there is something comforting about the fact that an eighteen-year-old may only be thirteen years old cognitively speaking. This statistic is a very valid reason for people to take advantage of bridge programs before college or to go to a community college for a few classes first before deciding on what they want to do with the rest of their lives. Understanding the cognitive development and emotional maturity of someone with ADHD can open a whole new world of possibilities both to those affected and to their loved ones.

When I was three months shy of my sixth birthday, my parents had me evaluated by a psychometrist, a doctor who studies mental capacity, at a learning disorders unit. Initially, I was diagnosed as "having problems with both activity level and acquisition of academic skills...[and] considered to be somewhat hyperactive." Although the conclusion of these tests dubbed me "a young man of average to above average overall intellectual ability," it was the last line of the doctor's report that would brand me forever:

"Behaviorally Leigh was hyperkinetic ...
His attention span is relatively short."

Did I mention that I was five?

One month later, in August of 1979, I found myself on a clinical trial of the stimulant medication, Ritalin. This jump seemed unfathomable at first. How could I have gone from being a little excitable to requiring Ritalin to simply get through kindergarten? What was the cause of this leap in treatment? Who was to blame? The answer:

Buck Rogers.

I was a science fiction lover from an early age. I loved fantasy, aliens, time travel, heroes and villains. In early 1979, a film, *Buck Rogers in the 25th Century*, was released. Of course I had to see it. My new Buck Rogers action figure was always at the ready to play out all the exciting new adventures featured in the film. My latest acquisition was the Buck Rogers Star Fighter spaceship. It was made of beautiful and pristine white plastic and was ready to sail through space and time. I loved it. That is, until I watched an episode of *Buck Rogers* and saw that the Star

Fighter had undergone severe fire damage. The "real" ship wasn't comprised of a flawless white material. No, the "real" ship was burned, singed, dirty-looking, and totally badass. I knew right then and there that my space ship had to look just like the "real" one on television.

When you're a kid with ADHD and you have the drive and determination to do something, there is very little that will stand in your way. In this case, the simple, rational concept that lighting something on fire was "bad" just didn't factor into my plan. So when, late one late August evening, I decided to make my Star Fighter look like it had been through the epic battle I had seen on television, I never thought that playing with fire was a bad idea or would be considered "trouble". I understood that fire was dangerous and kids weren't supposed to play with it, but this wasn't play. This was serious space business. The authentic, original Star Fighter had been burned, and mine would be too.

The logical place to have a star battle was the kitchen, so I crept downstairs in our apartment after I thought my mom was asleep. I knew that the Star Fighter did not have severe damage; it needed just a little singeing here and there to make it authentic. I found matches in our kitchen junk drawer and lit one. It went out surprisingly fast before I had a chance to do anything to my spaceship, so I tried again. I managed to melt a small spot on the Star Fighter, but it wasn't giving me that been-hit-in-intergalactic-warfare kind of look yet, so I knew I had to keep trying. I think it was on the third or fourth match that my mother emerged in the kitchen doorway. She was there just long enough to ascertain that I was lighting something on fire, and that was enough for her. Without questioning my motives, she screamed at me and quickly removed my toys and the matches from my possession. I sobbed as I tried to explain, but she wouldn't hear it, and I was sent to my room.

Less than a week later, I found myself in front of Dr. Smith, the pediatric neurologist, again. My mom had made a distress call to his office. My parents just didn't know what to do with my erratic and often irrational behavior. They felt very much at a loss for how to parent me. Their concern was genuine and necessary. Yet, for all of their concern, no one asked me why I was lighting matches in the kitchen at the age of five. No one wanted to hear my side of the story. This would become a trend throughout my childhood.

Dr. Smith's report of that visit states "He [Leigh] recently was caught setting fire to several objects in the first floor of his house in the middle of the night. We have started Leigh on Ritalin, which I hope will make a difference in his behavior as well as his activity level. It is entirely possible that we shall need to try him on lithium. We shall try to get him stabilized on a medication before school starts."

Did I mention that I was five?

CHAPTER TWO

THE SHORT BUS

Many parents of children with ADHD are not aware of all of the school-based resources that are available to their children. As a former teacher, Renee will admit that public schools don't necessarily readily provide special education (SPED) help because it is costly. In fact, a student with SPED support will cost roughly twice as much to educate as a student without those resources. It is understandable, from a school's perspective, why they would shrink from offering special education accommodations unless they are pressured or lawfully required to do so. This is why educating yourself on your child's rights as a student in the public school system is absolutely crucial. (Please note, I am not discussing private schools here because private schools do not even have to adhere to any of the laws regarding support for students with disabilities.)

First, you must know that you have every right to request an evaluation for special education services and/ or accommodations. This request is protected under the Individuals with Disabilities Education Act (IDEA) which, along with section 504 of the Rehabilitation Act, states that ADHD can be considered a disability. If your child has ADHD, or you think they might, and you feel that they are unable to achieve academic success because they are limited by their ADHD, then you may request an evaluation. At that point, the student may receive some sort of services. Depending on the severity of the student's ADHD and its impact on his or her ability to perform in school, a student can be given a 504 Plan or an Individualized Education Plan (IEP). There are significant distinctions between the two plans even though they are both designed to support and accommodate students with disabilities.

A 504 Plan is issued when a student does not qualify for a full IEP under the IDEA requirements, but who still requires assistance in the classroom. A 504 offers accommodations to the student, but they are limited to accommodations that can be administered by the classroom teacher. There are no legal requirements about what should be in a 504 Plan and the school is not even required to inform the parents that a 504 has been put into place, although most schools will contact the parents prior to implementing the accommodations. A 504 Plan covers students with any disability — any physical or mental condition that substantially limits a major life activity. Because of this loose definition, a 504 can apply to many different types of disabilities. For instance, a student with a severe allergy can qualify for 504 plan which states that he or she will be away from the allergen(s) and will outline a plan for what to do when/ if the student has a severe reaction. In order to receive a 504 Plan, a student's ADHD must somehow substantially limit his or her ability to perform a major life activity as it applies to school. For instance, someone with ADHD may struggle with copying notes down from the board onto their paper, so he might be provided with a copy of the teacher's notes in accordance with the 504.

If a person's ADHD is severe enough to hinder their ability to learn in a regular classroom, he may be eligible for an IEP plan under the term "Other Heath Impairment" (OHI). They might also have an additional condition that causes them to struggle in the classroom, such as a Specific Learning Disability (SLD) or a Severe Emotional Disturbance (SED). When a student falls under this level of impairment, the IEP is presented and followed through by the special education department (SPED). An IEP gives students an additional layer of assistance, not only because of the accommodations it can provide, but because they have a SPED or inclusion teacher who helps manage and assess their work. An IEP is a legal document and certain regulations must be followed. It contains information about the student's personalized goals and services provided to him or her. The plan and the child's progress are monitored throughout the school year, and the IEP itself must be reviewed and renewed annually.

It is important to know that not all people with ADHD will qualify for either plan. According to the Americans with Disabilities Act (ADA), in order for ADHD to be considered a disability, it must cause "a physical or mental impairment that substantially limits one or more major life activities" (*U.S. Department of Labor*). Although the list is not exhaustive, these activities "include, but are not limited to, caring for oneself, performing manual tasks, seeing, hearing, eating, sleeping, walking, standing, lifting, bending, speaking, breathing, learning, reading, concentrating, thinking, communicating, and working" (*U.S. Department of Labor*). The list is thorough, but it is certainly broad and open for interpretation in some areas. Most students with ADHD find that their ability to learn like a neuro-typical, or non-ADHD, person in a school environment is next to impossible without the help of some accommodations. Therefore, I would argue that ADHD should qualify a student, at the very least, for a 504 Plan and possibly even an IEP, depending on how the ADHD influences her brain and her behavior.

Sometimes it is hard for parents to get past the notion that their child may require special education. SPED had a different stigma in my youth than it does now, but parents often cringe at the notion of their child being singled out or labeled. When these parents approach Renee and say that they don't want them to have to be placed in special education, Renee asks them a fairly simple question: "If you had all of the necessary resources to help your child be successful, wouldn't you want to use them?" It is hard to say "no" to this question. Of course we all want our children to be successful in school, as in anything else they set out to accomplish. When you put it that way, it just makes sense for parents to inquire about a 504 or an

IEP plan. Children can outgrow the need for an IEP, but they will never grow out of their ADHD.

If it were not for Section 504 of the Rehabilitation Act of 1973, I may have had a very different life. This section guarantees a "'free appropriate public education' (FAPE) to each qualified person with a disability who is in the school district's jurisdiction, regardless of the nature or severity of the person's disability" ("Free Appropriate…"). That is a lot of verbiage to sort through, but essentially this means that all children, whether they are disabled or not, are entitled to equal public education. Equal does not mean that they are to be given the exact same education, but that the public education in place must meet the individual student's needs. Although this law has been in place since 1973, it isn't one that people would necessarily know unless they were directly affected by it.

My parents were directly affected by it.

First grade marked the start of my long line of academic failures. It was barely mid-year before my parents were receiving daily phone calls to pick me up from school. I was described as "disruptive", "unable to sit still", "impulsive" and "hyperkinetic". However, teachers and schools at the time were so uneducated about ADHD that they did not realize that I exhibited normal behavior — for a boy with ADHD. Therefore, the school began to tell my mom to keep me home for a

day, or a week, or even two weeks. I wasn't suspended. I was just asked to "take a break".

While this greatly upset my parents, what truly pushed the situation over the edge was when they received a letter home from the school's principal. The letter explained that my first grade teacher's husband had recently passed away. Her mental state was described as "fragile", and the principal informed my parents that she should not have to "put up with Leigh" during this time. My parents weren't aware that this letter's suggestion was entirely illegal, but they did know that something had to change.

In the spring of 1979, I should have been finishing first grade year. Instead, I was removed from the public school and placed in a different type of school that was supposed to help me mature. I'm not sure whose idea it was for me to do this extra year, but what is certain is that this year did not do anything to ensure my scholastic success. It just made me a year older and further behind than ever. I did not yet realize I had been labeled as different. In fact, I thought I was pretty special, considering there was a bus coming around my neighborhood that was just for me.

One morning, I was sitting in front our RCA Roundy color television set watching an episode of *Star Blazers*. Suddenly, I heard a great deal of heavy-handed car horn noises coming from the street. I reluctantly began making my way outside as I muttered and mumbled about not wanting to go to school. The horn ruckus was coming from the transportation to my new school — a 1977 Ford LTD Country Squire station wagon with a school bus sign shoddily screwed onto the roof. The driver was a heavy-set woman with long, brown, greasy hair, parted in the middle. That day she was wearing jeans and a light blue flannel shirt that was worn through the elbows. She never acknowledged my existence. She never wished me good morning at pick up, and never told me to have a good day at drop off. In fact, I never even knew if she was capable of smiling.

I sat in the front, middle seat. To my right was a boy about my age. I found it odd that he was wearing a helmet on the bus. The helmet had a make-shift guard on the front that made me think that he was ready for a street hockey game. I guessed he just wanted to be prepared for anything. His constant smile assured me that he was friendly enough, so I figured we would be instant friends. Always the clown, I started to tell jokes that probably made no sense, but my new buddy seemed to think that I was hilarious so I kicked back and began to enjoy the trip to school.

We reached a stoplight at an intersection downtown. Just as the light was turning green, three women began to cross the intersection in front of our "bus". Apparently our driver did not believe that pedestrians should have the right of way and she rolled down her window and yelled at them to hurry up. The women attempting to cross the intersection were clearly irritated by being told to hurry up and they approached the driver's side window of the station wagon. One of the women grabbed our bus driver by her hair through the window and tugged her entire head out of the car. While our driver twisted, turned, and howled, the other woman punched her face repeatedly. Although the beating probably lasted thirty seconds or so, it was the longest, most fascinating thirty seconds of my short life. Finally, our driver managed to pull her head back into the automobile and step on the gas. She sped through the intersection, bleeding out of her nose and side of her mouth.

My hockey-masked friend began to cry and his whimper quickly turned into a loud sob. I couldn't think of a joke to cheer him up, and his screaming eventually became unbearable. Our driver veered suddenly to the right and slammed on the brakes. Then she began to cry as well. I didn't know what to do, so I stated the obvious. "Uh oh! We're going to be late for school!" I blurted. Our driver instantly stopped crying and glared at me. She reached behind her, grabbed me by my shirt, and pulled me into the front seat toward her. Her cigarette breath was rancid, as were her yellowed, bloody teeth. I could barely breathe as she glared at me and then she screamed,

"I don't fucking care if you're going to be late for school! I'll be damned if I keep wasting my life chauffeuring around a bunch of retards!" She let go of me and turned her attention back to driving.

I almost agreed with her. No one should "waste their life". Then I realized that she was looking at me. Me. I was one of the "retards". That was what people thought of me. Me, in my short bus. The notion was shocking, confusing, and hurtful. I wanted to scream at her that we weren't "retards" and that we would show her. I wanted to tell her that we would amount to something and that we were unique and special. I wanted to tell her that I

13

was just repeating kindergarten to become more mature, and not because there was anything "wrong" with me.

I wanted to tell her all these things and more, but, at that point, I don't know if I believed any of them anymore.

My friend in the hockey mask was no longer crying. He looked at me and smiled.

CHAPTER THREE

NOT-SO-SMOOTH SAILING

E veryone lies at some point in his life. Whether it is a small white lie or a big orchestrated tale, it doesn't matter because a lie is a lie. What does matter, however, is the reason behind the lie in the first place. Frequent lying can be a common trait for those with ADHD, and it can be enormously frustrating for the people who are being lied to. That said, understanding the reason behind the lie can be enormously helpful. Most of the time people lie because they are stressed, fearful, or they are simply trying to avoid repercussions. While ADHDers might lie for any of the aforementioned reasons, there may also be something else at work.

As I have already discussed, the ADHD brain develops differently than a neurotypical brain. The developmental delay in many tasks associated with executive functioning tends to be roughly three to three and a half years. If we accept this developmental delay as accurate, which most doctors now do, it is entirely possible to argue that an

ADHD youth's prefrontal cortex is too immature to sort through the consequences of telling a lie. Additionally, we must also remember that impulsivity, one of the major characteristic traits of ADHD, is often the reason that one tells a lie. Hence, without even digging very far, we have already uncovered two legitimate and valid reasons why someone with ADHD might tell a lie. If we then add in a person's natural tendency towards self-preservation, we may not have to ask ourselves why ADHDers lie, but rather marvel at how they ever manage to tell the truth!

In a recent vlog, Renee discussed an alternative way to look at the cause of telling a lie. She said, "Think about it from the flip side. What does my child perceive the repercussions to be if he or she tells the truth? What do they think will happen if they admit wrongdoing?" Furthermore, she asked the parents to think about what children might be afraid of. This mindset is difficult for some parents because it forces them to be self-reflective and to think about their role in their child's lies. Many parents are resistant to this because they do not want to take any ownership for their child's misbehavior. To them, lies are wrong and the reason behind them is simplified to an attempt to avoid getting into trouble. But I would ask them, and you, to think about what it looks like when a child "gets into trouble." What is it about their punishment that they fear so much that they perceive lying about it is a better option? What if we realized that our ADHD children are so broken down by negative words, gestures, grades, social interactions, etc., that they simply cannot stand yet another blow? What if the lie is unwittingly designed to make you, as the parent, proud of the child because he or she craves that positive attention so desperately? If we think about it from this perspective, it could entirely change how we parent in certain situations.

In 1979 we were living in a two-family, two-story rental home and things were not going well. My father was pumping gas and going to school, and my mother was waitressing the third shift at a restaurant. The stress of our tight budget and my parents' attempts to deal with me had taken a toll on everyone. My mother and father worked tirelessly to give my brother and I everything we needed, but we were left alone a great deal. Naturally, I took advantage of being left to my own devices quite often.

One fall afternoon after school I was feeling especially antsy. I knew I had to get out. My window had no screen, did not lock, and was conveniently located in the back of the house, three feet off the ground. Climbing out of it was almost as easy as walking out the front door.

I landed on the ground outside of my window and walked around the corner of the house to where there was a staircase leading up to our back deck. Underneath the stairs among tall, over-grown grass sat a box of matches that I had previously stashed. There was something satisfying about lighting things on fire, and I tried to experiment with it every chance I got. I didn't have a plan for this afternoon, but I knew my matches would play a crucial part.

I jogged towards the tree line at the back of our house. This small wooded section of communal property separated the homes on my street from a large open field, and on the other side of that field was a five-story apartment building. The open field was mostly grass, except for a large sand mound just off center of the rectangular shaped field. It was a place that I loved. School continued to be challenging, our neighborhood was a harsh, unforgiving place made up of elementary school drug dealers and relentless bullies, and my family was in shambles. I felt at peace outside exploring the field on my own. The idea that I was also doing something that I wasn't supposed to be doing elevated my enjoyment of these moments.

I trudged along through the field, blue tip matchbox under my left arm, searching the ground for things that I could test for flammability. I was growing discouraged by the lack of discarded trash, so I walked closer to the apartment building on the other side of the field. The edge of the building's grayish cement parking lot greeted me. Since it was about four in the afternoon, there were only a few cars dispersed throughout the lot. My eyes caught sight of a blue Volkswagen Beetle a few paces away, and something white was reflecting the sun the back seat of the car. I walked closer, casually looking to see if anyone else was around, but I was alone. Once I was just a few feet away from the Beetle, I looked into the backseat and saw an intricate, model sailboat. The boat itself was nearly one foot long. As I admired the handiwork, another thought popped into my head "That boat would look awesome if it was lit on fire!"

Impulsively, I tried the handle of the backdoor to the car and it easily popped open. I grabbed the sailboat and quickly shut the door behind me. Giddily, I ran back towards the middle of the field. I set the sailboat down in the grass and lifted my box of matches from its slightly damp nook in my armpit. I wedged the bottom of the ship into the ground a bit so that, between that and the blades of grass surrounding it, the ship stood upright as if it were about to embark on its maiden voyage across the grass field. I counted aloud "1, 2, 3…"—struck a match and then held the flame to the end of the sail closest to me.

Like all things when they are lit on fire, the sail caught the flame slowly at first and then gradually the yellowish-orange tongue took over. The flame consumed the sail as I had hoped it would, but it also dropped fiery ashes onto the flimsy plywood-like bottom of the ship. To my delight, the entire model sailboat was ablaze in less than one minute. In my head I played out an entire epic battle in which a plane overhead dropped a bomb on the enemy sailboat. The imaginary people aboard were screaming for their lives, cursing the bombers in the unseen plane in the sky, the ship was sinking, engulfing their cries as the fire grew stronger and larger, and then…

The grass caught on fire.

It happened quickly, but the flame didn't disperse as rapidly as it had with the readily flammable cloth sails and faux-wood boat. It did, however, begin to creep from one blade to the next and then to the next. Logic should have told me to stomp on the burning ground, but logic and I rarely saw eye-to-eye, so instead, I grabbed the charred remains of the model boat and I ran. I ran back home, through the trees, to my window, and hoisted myself back up into my room. I shut the window and threw myself onto my bed, breathing heavily with a mix of fear, exhaustion, and exhilaration.

Shortly after returning home, a fire truck's siren blared nearby. I wanted to go outside and watch them put out the fire. I couldn't believe how cool it was that the fire department had been called all on account of me! But I knew I couldn't go watch, and as I heard my mom's steps in the hallway, I went to stand near the window and tried to will the trees that blocked my line of sight away. The sirens only lasted a couple of minutes. I assumed the fire had been stopped quickly and that that would be that. However, as it neared 7pm that evening, a heavy-handed knock rattled our front door.

I had not emerged from my room, except to grab a sandwich for dinner about an hour earlier. From behind my closed door, I could hear a muffled deep voice that I knew did not belong to my dad. "Leigh!" my mother's voice echoed down the hallway. "Come out here now!" I obeyed fearlessly, until I got to our front door and saw two local police officers blocking the entryway. "These men want to ask you about a fire in the field today," my mom said flatly. I shrugged. My mind raced even faster than it normally races, as I tried to think through how or why they would possibly connect me to the fire. But I knew that trouble followed me as fast as I followed it so I was not surprised to be summoned for questioning.

"Hello young man," the taller of the two officers said as he bent slightly at the waist to get closer to my eye-level. "I wonder if you know anything about the fire that occurred this afternoon?" I could only shake my head to indicate "no". He stood up straight and I thought, for once, someone had believed me right away, but then he bent down farther, "One of your neighbors seems to think they saw you carrying something that looked pretty burned earlier. Maybe a toy boat of some kind." I waited for my mom to tell them that I didn't have a toy boat, but she looked tight-lipped and angry.

"I found that in the trash!" I blurted. I had no idea where that answer came from.

"You found what in the trash?"

"The boat. It was uh…burned. I thought it looked cool so I took it. From the trash." I mumbled, hiding ever so slightly behind the open front door. I could feel the four eyes of the police officers penetrating my soul. I dared not look up because my mother would know by the tiniest twinkle in my eye or unintentional smirk on my face that I was lying. I heard a sigh and the movement of fabric caused by a shift in weight and arms crossing across a chest.

"The trash, huh?" I nodded, keeping my eyes on the floor. I waited. I nearly thrust my arms outward willingly and screamed for them to just "take me in!", but I waited and waited. "All right. I guess that's it then," the officer said. My head snapped to attention. "Good night folks." And with that, they turned and strutted out the door. Finally, I let my smile widen as I watched them get into their police car and slowly pull away from in front of our house. I turned, expecting to see my mother's knowing glare, but she had already left the doorway and was heading to her bedroom mumbling something about being late for work. I stifled a chuckle of glee and shut the front door.

I had lied. I had lied to the police. I had lied to the police *and* I had gotten away with it. Who knew where the boundaries were now? But it didn't really matter. I was going to test them no matter what.

CHAPTER FOUR

THE DARKEST OF (SNOW) DAYS

The content of the following story contains adult themes and events. Renee and I strongly recommend that, if you have a child reading this book along with you, you skip this next story for now. We do, however, believe that it needs to be told and we ask that you come back and read it on your own.

My wife and I wanted to write this book to bring hope, suggestions, and inspiration to people with or people affected by ADHD. We want to change the way the world thinks about ADHD. Our message has always been a positive one so we sought to tell anecdotes that would illustrate how ADHD could be used as a strength, even if it takes a long time to figure out how to use it in such a way. Although we have tried to use humor and lightheartedness to tell many of these memories, there are some stories that should not be sugar coated. This is one of them.

Renee and I searched for information and studies

to throw into the introduction to this piece. There are statistics out there but we just aren't sure that the ones we found are truly valid or that they necessarily bring anything to the table. The most recent and seemingly truthful information comes from a 2015 study at the University of Toronto. This study attempted to find a correlation between ADHD and experiencing sexual abuse. It states:

> Among women, 34 percent of those with ADHD reported they were sexually abused before they turned 18. In contrast, 14 percent of women without ADHD reported that they had experienced childhood sexual abuse… Fuller-Thomson's research also noted that a greater percentage of men with ADHD than men without ADHD reported that they were sexually abused (11 percent vs six percent) or physically abused (41 per cent vs 31 per cent) during their childhood. (Staff, Science)

What is troublesome to me is that there is no hard evidence or explanation given as to why someone with ADHD would have a greater chance of being sexually abused than someone without. The only possible reason that we found is that a person with ADHD is more impulsive and therefore potentially more likely to put him or herself into an unfavorable situation or environment, but that seems inadequate. While we may not understand the repercussions of our actions, this doesn't explain how males with ADHD could end up with a 5% higher likelihood of sexual abuse. Sexual abuse requires an abuser, and even if we blame our own impulsivity for getting us into precarious situations, this doesn't explain how we could be that much more likely to be around someone perverted enough to abuse.

I don't put much stock in studies as a whole, but I do put stock in life experience. I believe there is much to learn from listening to others. I know I have found inspiration in other people's success stories and in how they persevered when the chips were down. I hope people can learn something from mine.

Going to elementary school means living for snow days. When a snow day happens it is an unexpectedly joyous occasion that results in a fun-filled day with friends. That is what my seven-year-old self expected from this winter weekday off of school, but that is not what I got. What I got was an experience that would scar me emotionally and physically in a way that I never thought possible. It would be a snow day that I would never forget.

In the winter of 1980, I spent a lot of time with Mandy. On top of my reputation as a trouble-causing, hyper, strange boy, I had recently started having seizures which were frightening and often gruesome to watch. Mandy was one of the few kids I knew that was not completely disgusted by my presence. We often watched MTV at her house or played outside in the streets, the neighboring fields, or in a small brook. She tolerated me and I welcomed any sort of friendship, so we were a good pair. On that fateful snow day it made sense that we would find one another and decide to spend the day playing together.

With my parents both working full-time, I had carte blanche. Most of the families around us were also dual-income working class families who felt safe in allowing their children to go outside at day break and go unaccounted for until dark. Various children emerged to play in the snow, which had stopped falling during the early morning hours.

Mandy and I met in front of her house and began a short trek to a small stream next to an old, dilapidated barn along a nearby road. The wooden barn was small and shack-like. It sat back tucked behind trees and open land about 450 yards away from the street. It may have been painted white at one time, but by then was a weathered grey color. The barn was held up by four cubical wooden stilts driven deep into the ground at all four of the structure's corners. This elevated the shed about one foot off of the ground. On one side of the barn was an empty field and, on the other side, was the tiny brook. This small body of water weaved its way past the back of the barn, perpendicular to the road and eventually collided and disappeared into the street. The area was secluded and I'd loved the adventures I had there. With its old appearance and slightly hidden location, the barn was not a place where parents frequented, so all of us kids took comfort in calling this our treehouse or our fort.

On this particular snow day, the stream that ran past the back of the barn was fully frozen in some parts and still thawed and moving along in others. It was no surprise that Mandy's older brother, Eric, and two of his friends joined us there shortly after we arrived. Eric was easily the largest out of the three of them. His age, his size, and his capacity to bully people normally intimidated me, but on that day we seemed to all be friends. At the tender age of seven, the idea of hanging out with older, cooler companions was exciting, and I eagerly accepted their company by the brook.

We poked sticks through the ice, watched the water whoosh through underneath the frozen parts, dared each other to walk across this or that flimsy section of ice. We were kids with a snow day and it was glorious. Eventually, we made our way to the barn. The five of us went inside. The barn was full of someone's trash. It wasn't garbage though, although there were remnants of wrappers from our past visits there. It contained many pieces of unwanted wood and other building materials that someone must have abandoned when they relocated. We all gathered a few pieces of wood from around the barn, but they all were slightly damp due to the wetness hanging in the air. When enough scraps were collected, we sat around a duct work tube that we'd found and took turns striking matches into the fire. The crumbled newspaper we had burned too quickly and did not allow the wood pieces enough time to catch fire. The boys fumbled with the matches and continued to try to set the blaze without success. Mandy grew cold and tired of waiting, so she headed home. I was thoroughly engrossed in a broken piece of banister railing that I picked up. There were crayons stashed in the barn from a previous visit, and I found the blue one. I colored one end of the smooth stick blue. It was going to be my Light Saber!

As I furiously colored away, I started to get a familiar grinding feeling. A small buzzing sensation crept into the back of my eyes and throat and suddenly I felt very itchy in my own skin. I knew a seizure was coming. I began to lose my sense of depth perception, and I felt a lack of control over my body. I fell over onto my side from the cross-legged seated position I had been in as I colored my light saber. I blacked out—I don't know for how long. All I knew was, when I came to, one of Eric's friends was sitting on my back.

As with any seizure, even a small one such as this, I felt weak when I reopened my eyes and I had little control over my own motor function. The boy on my back weighed enough that I could not get up off of my stomach, which was pushed down hard into the dampened floorboards. As I struggled helplessly, I felt someone tugging on my pants. I cried out some wordless noise and then a boot came down squarely onto my face. The kick was hard, and it both surprised and stung me. I hadn't seen it coming and could only imagine that it was from the other one of Eric's friends. Eric, himself, had another agenda.

He had pulled my pants and underwear down just past

my knees. He placed his own knees in between my legs, pinning down my pants and rendering my legs useless in the struggle. I strained my neck to look behind me but the boy on my back prevented me from turning to see the horror that was about to unfold. Eric picked up the piece of banister I had been holding and forced the end into my rectum. A pain like no other I had experienced shot through my rear end and rippled throughout the rest of my body. I screamed "Noooooooo!" and felt something hit me on the back of the head. I struggled to get out from under the boy on my back and to get my legs untangled from my pants and underwear, but I did not have the strength to stop the torture.

The stick probed deeper into my anal cavity as Eric leaned more weight on it. I cried and yelled, "Help!" and "Stop!" but it was useless. The intense pain in my bottom was only interrupted by slaps and kicks to my head or face when I yelled. Intermingled amongst their laughter I heard,

"Shut up, Spaz!" and I realized that this was my torment for being different. I wailed for them to stop and was met by a kick to the face. I picked my head up off the ground and turned it to the right to at least get my face away from whoever's boot that was, but then I felt a harder kick to the back of my head. For a brief instant, a white light the color of the snow that gave us that miserable day off clouded my vision. Then, it was gone and I was back staring at the wall of the barn through my puffy right eye as my left eye was crushed against the floor. Between the seizure, the beatings, and the assault on one of my most private of areas, I had no sense of time or awareness of anything besides pain. Suddenly though, and seemingly without warning, the three boys just stopped. The beater stopped beating. The holder stopped holding. The raper stopped raping. They ran, giddily, out the door of the barn and disappeared into the whiteness.

My senses half-returned as my face swelled from the kicks and I felt a complete chill run through my body. The coldness of the wooden floor seeped into my exposed face, my genitals and my quadriceps. With my pants down around my shins, I tried to pull my knees into my chest so I could get up onto them and put my underwear and clothes back on, but every time I turned my body slightly in one direction or another I was met with sharp pain in my rectum. The stick was still wedged inside me. I sobbed quietly. There was no sense in crying loudly anymore because clearly no one could hear me. No one had come to my rescue. I took a deep breath, reached around to grab what was once going to be my superhero light saber, and pulled once. It didn't move. I pulled harder. There came a brief, immobilizing, tearing pain through my insides, and the banister finally came loose.

My hands, which had been wet from wiping my tears, were now wet with the blood that oozed out of my rectum. I turned myself over and sat up. One of my Velcro Zips shoes was missing. I removed the other one and shimmed my way out of my pants. They were partially wet from our adventures in the brook and I had to struggle to get them the rest of the way down my legs. I took my underwear off too and used it as a make-shift towel to wipe the blood that drizzled from my bottom. As I cleaned myself off, I refused to accept the gravity of what had happened. Disoriented, confused, and physically and mentally wounded, I put my pants and my one shoe back on and willed myself to get up.

I couldn't. Although the pain was intense, it wasn't what kept me sitting in that dilapidated barn. I wiped my hands on my dirtied underwear and I felt as dirty as the stains that were left behind. I could not understand *what* had happened, let alone why. Why had Mandy left me there alone with those boys? Why had they tormented me? Why was I subjected to such cruelty? My head was still foggy from the seizure and the blows to the face, but even as clarity began to set in, I still did not have answers to those questions. The only thing I was sure of is that I'd woken up to a nightmare. A humiliating, degrading, life-altering assault from which I did not know how to recover. As I sat in the barn, growing colder and more and more filled with shame, I realized something terrible. I could not tell anyone about what happened.

It was not that I wanted to protect those horrid boys or that I was mortified to tell someone what they had done. It was that I knew, even at the age of seven, that no one would believe me. I was a liar. Everyone knew me to be a liar. Why would they believe this story, which seemed even more unrealistic and outlandish than any lie I could ever come up with? I could not think of anyone who would believe me. Perhaps I could have gone to a guidance counselor or teacher, but my past experiences with them were all negative. Perhaps I could have gone to a friend, but I didn't have many and I certainly didn't want the friends I did have to think I was any weirder than they already did. Perhaps I could have gone to my parents, but the thought that they might not believe me was too much to bear. Also, everyone in my life knew that I was a "bad" kid. This realization was perhaps the most painful of all. With the enormity of that unthinkable secret on my seven-year-old shoulders, I took a deep breath, stood up, and walked out of the barn door, down our drawbridge, and back towards the stream.

Every step electrified the pain in my anus. I was sure I was scratched by the stick as much on my inside as I had been on the outside. With each foot forward, I could feel raw skin rub against raw skin as I made my way back the way we came. In my left hand, I held my bloodied underwear. I felt like I had to bring them home, but I couldn't explain away the blood so, instead, I wadded them up into a ball and threw them across the stream. Then, in a small moment of triumph, I spotted my other sneaker laying on top of the snow on the side of the water. I retrieved it, not caring about how wet my pants or feet got. At that point, it didn't matter. Nothing mattered except getting that sneaker.

The tale of that snow day would be mine and mine alone until many years later when, as an awkward teenager, I would finally tell my mother. I told her an abbreviated, mild version of the sexual assault. I wish I could say that I told her because I wanted to open up and trust in her, but that wasn't the case. I told her flippantly to distract her from something else. I downplayed it all. I realize now, only in retrospect, that this was because I was still consumed with shame. She was devastated. She wept because she felt that she had not been there for me. But my seventh year spanned a time when I was often in trouble at school. At home, my parents were constantly arguing about what to do with me. It was even suggested to them that they put me into a foster home or institutionalize me. I don't think my mother realized that by simply keeping me under their roof, she had been there for me. I am enormously thankful that my parents did not go down the alternative placement road, but I don't think I have ever told them that.

CHAPTER FIVE

THE BAD NEWS BEAR

One might be surprised to learn that 75% of persons with ADHD will be diagnosed with an additional condition at some point in their lives. These conditions can range from learning disabilities to bipolar disorder. Anxiety, depression, sleep disorders, and Oppositional Defiant Disorder are especially common. I don't know what to make of these connections other than the fact that many of their symptoms seem to overlap with the symptoms of ADHD. I know I have fought off depressed thoughts now and then but I don't believe that I *have* depression. Do I believe that having ADHD can sometimes *be* depressing? Absolutely.

You don't have to be a scientist or do a lot of research to realize that someone with ADHD struggles in certain aspects of his or her life. When this struggle is not properly understood by the people in the ADHDer's life, (and even sometimes when it is understood and sympathized with), that person's existence can be filled with negative experiences. Think of all the times you, as someone with ADHD, have done something "wrong". Perhaps you were late to an important meeting because of your time insensitivity. Maybe you were too blunt with a neighbor during a discussion about lawn upkeep. Perhaps you were given instructions, but you just didn't listen to them and then you failed at the task you were supposed to do. Maybe you spent all of your money impulsively and plunged your family into credit card debit. The possibilities are endless. What do these struggles result in? Negative reinforcement. I know from experience what this can do to one's self-esteem. My entire childhood was cloaked in discussions about what I did wrong, what I should not do, what I would never be able to do, etc. How is it possible to remain upbeat when the outside world views you so poorly? It took me a long time to figure that out. Although it is a difficult, uphill struggle, it *is* possible. I hope you can figure it out too.

My doctors always recommended that I do something physical to help with my hyperactivity. Playing sports is a great way for ADHD kids and adults to work out anxiety and extra energy. Most kids my age played baseball. My parents thought this classic sport would be the ideal solution not only for burning off my energy, but also to help me gain some confidence and possibly some social skills by forcing me to interact with other kids on a team.

Baseball did not come naturally to me. I did not have the hand-eye coordination necessary to hit or catch. I could throw adequately, but getting me to pay attention long enough for another player to hit the ball was beyond challenging. Due to my poor skills, I was usually relegated to the outfield, where I could space out accordingly.

People often confuse the desire to do something with the ability to something. I had the desire to be a productive member of a team, just as I had the desire to be a decent student and a well-behaved child. I simply lacked the *ability* to be those things. It wasn't because I could not do them, but because I didn't have the necessary tools to be able to understand *how* to do them. Some people would insist that medication is an effective tool and I don't disagree, but medication without direction is not beneficial and only leads to failure. Which leads to more medication. It's a vicious cycle that I was stuck in for nearly thirteen years, and I wouldn't wish it on anyone.

I remember one particular game that really solidified the notion that baseball was not going to solve my issues. Even though I was no Babe Ruth, I was not the worst player on the team—or so I thought. During this game I got to play the coveted position of shortstop. The shortstop gets a lot of action. This was a huge step up from playing in the outfield, where I was accustomed to taking up residence. Jogging out to shortstop with my head held high, I knew I had the desire to be successful. I wanted to show everyone that I was good enough to have earned that spot.

Unfortunately, desire and ability do not go hand in hand. A few missed pop-ups and ground balls were enough to start the heckling from the sidelines. I wish I could say that it was the other team that heckled me, but, in fact, it was the parents from *my* team that were the worst. They were not kind, nor did they try to hide their distaste for the coach's choice to put me in at shortstop. I suppose this should have really hurt my feelings, but, I was accustomed to this type of ridicule. However, it didn't make things any easier when I was switched back to outfield.

The demotion would have been easier to swallow had it not been for my replacement. I mean, I knew I did not have a future in the major leagues, but when the coach called the girl from right field in to switch her to short stop, my heart sank. She had one arm. In order to be a fielder, she had to catch the ball in her glove, get her hand out of the glove, place it on the ground, grab the ball with her one hand, and then throw it. Despite all of this, she was undeniably better than I was at baseball. She legitimately had more talent in her one hand than I had in both of mine.

This girl had a real, visible disability but she did not let that stop her. She was positive and energetic and she had figured out what I had yet to learn. She had figured out that if she wanted to be successful, she had to put in more work and effort than the average person. Was this unfair? Unjust? Sure. Did that matter to her? Nope. At her young age, she had already learned how to work with her disability. I, on the other hand, was at a complete loss for how my mind worked. And so, it made perfect sense that she should usurp my position because she was better than me in every possible way.

This moment was symbolic for my life as a whole.

Even though the insults and embarrassment fueled my desire to do better, I lacked the ability to succeed because I did not know how. Success was a foreign concept to me because no one ever told me that I *could* succeed. Putting me at shortstop when I lacked the ability to play was just setting me up for failure. Rather than encouraging me and boosting my confidence, playing Little League just showed everyone that I was incapable of being "normal". This sentiment would be reinforced throughout my life, but no one realized the vicious cycle that was created. Where other children got guidance and encouragement for how to be successful, I got more medication. I got more reasons *why* I couldn't do things and less explanations for *how to* do things. I didn't know how to articulate what I needed from people at this point in my life. I just knew that I was disappointed that those around me seemed determined to do the exact opposite of what I needed them to do. I also knew that I could never, ever tell them this because it would seem argumentative, and I was determined to fly under the radar and stay as far away from Dr. Smith as possible. Instead, I wallowed silently and chalked the baseball debacle up to another time I had let people down. There seemed to be no end to my misery.

CHAPTER SIX

THE STATEMENT

Dr. Edward Hallowell describes ADHD as "having a powerful race car for a brain, but with bicycle brakes" (Hallowell, Edward "ADHD Overview"). This metaphor is extremely fitting. An ADHD brain moves fast and it is difficult to stop. This leads to impulsivity and/or the inability to filter out distracting stimuli. While I concur with this description of ADHD, it's time to urge people to stop seeing all of the characteristics of ADHD as negative and start seeing the positives that can come from a "race car brain".

While it might be tempting to complain that ADHD causes us to be distracted, instead, let us look at the benefits of distractibility. Invention and creativity can emerge from a seemingly distracted brain. The constant whirlwind in our brains can result in new and innovative ideas. I would argue that most out of the box thinking comes from people with ADHD because we are bored with the "normal" ways, and therefore we seek alternative routes and solutions. Albert Einstein and Walt Disney were both believed to have had ADHD. Imagine what we would have missed out on if their brains had slowed down!

Surely there can't be any benefits to being hyperactive, right? Wrong! Channeling that extra energy in a positive way can be a recipe for success. Enthusiasm, spontaneity, and excitement are all things that you can expect with spending time with an ADHDer. While many sources of information may paint hyperactivity in a negative light, the constant need to be in motion can result in drive and determination unlike that of a "normal" brain. For me, this itch to move is what propels me to be successful in the field of sales. If I were to grow tired or wear out, I would not have the motivation and incentive to press on, make more calls, visit more stores, or continue to educate myself on how I can improve on what I already do well. Frankly, I would have given up a long time ago had it not been for the motor inside my body that drives me to go, go, go. Michael Phelps, Jim Carrey, and Justin Timberlake are just a few of the well-known celebrities with ADHD who have reached extraordinary heights because of their drive and energy.

Occasionally, the ADHD brain's motor gets stuck on one gear. This is when hyperfocus can occur. We become unable to move past a certain thought or task until we accomplish or conquer whatever task or thought it is that consumes our mind. If left unattended, hyper focus can monopolize your life. It can take the form of fear that can grow into anxiety or it can become obsessive and control your every move. Hyperfocus, like distractibility and hyperactivity, is often viewed in a negative light. However, it has its advantages. I may hyperfocus on something that needs to be done for work, or, I daresay, I may have even hyperfocused on completing this book. This unrelenting thought pattern means that I will do everything in my power to learn everything there is to learn about the object of my focus, and I will do everything in my power to complete, overcome, tackle, or achieve whatever it is that I am obsessing about. Hyperfocus only dissipates when something more interesting occurs, or when whatever you've been hyperfocused on is accomplished. Entrepreneurs Richard Branson and Charles Schwab are good examples of how ADHD hyperfocus can be beneficial. Without it, these great men may not have set their minds on developing a business or a brand.

There are many other strengths that come from having ADHD. My hope is that this book will help educate people on the positive aspects of Attention Deficit Hyperactive Disorder. For forty-three years, people have told me what is wrong with me. I think it's time you were told what is right.

It was a perfectly average day in the fall of 1983. Then again, most days seemed average from the top floor of our duplex. My parents were blue collar, hardworking folks. My father had just finished college and was a staff accountant at a grocery company. Prior to that, he pumped gas at a local station. My mother worked the night shift as a waitress at a local chain restaurant while she went to school part-time for clinical psychology in the hopes of becoming a social worker someday. Although we lived meagerly, my parents had aspirations to better themselves and the lives of their children. I, too, had aspirations. I was going to be a spy. I was simultaneously immersed in the television worlds of "Get Smart" and "Doctor Who", and I was convinced that I was going to be an intergalactic spy who helped aliens save the world. As a ten-year-old, I obviously lacked credentials. Clearly, I needed to hone my detection capabilities. I needed to improve upon my stealth. I needed to—well—to *spy*!

My mother worked the third shift so she was always home when I got home from school. She managed the afternoons of homework and after school play time for me and my brother on her own. Play time outside could get a little dicey. Going outside meant possibly contending with gang members so my brother and I were often left to our own, in-house devices rather than to negotiate the child-Mafia activities outside our walls. On this particular day my mom had her friend Dennis over for tea (or perhaps for something stronger). She and Dennis were good friends and my mom trusted and confided in him.

After my brother was put to bed for the night, Dennis and my mom settled down to chat in the cramped living room of our apartment. They thought I was in my room for the night as well, but I had other plans. In my mind, it was the perfect spy gig; two unsuspecting people exchanging pertinent information that was too secretive and too private for young ears. Behind the closed doors of my bedroom, I picked up my tape recorder and rewound the tape to the beginning. Donning a secret agent-worthy pair of tighty-whities, I began the short army crawl to the living room. The adults were deep in conversation and did not hear my slow, quiet slither to the side of the room. The short, worn carpet made the approach quick and easy for the super spy I felt I was quickly becoming. I gently pushed the tape recorder by its handle into position underneath the end table nearest the hallway. I held my breath. Slowly and unobtrusively, I pushed down the red button marked "Record". Success! I exhaled with relief.

It was only when I was trying to figure out how to back out of the room without banging my head on the underside of the end table that I heard my name. I froze. They'd caught me. I was a failure, again. However, it turns out that my mother wasn't scolding me or catching me in the spy act. No, she was talking *about* me. "We just don't know what to do about Leigh," she was saying. "Doctor Smith isn't even sure how to proceed." My ears tingled at the name of my pediatrician. Dr. Smith wasn't your typical pediatrician. He was training in pediatrics and neurology with a specialty in learning disorders at a nationally acclaimed children's hospital. He had taken a special interest in me from a young age, and I had been under his care for four years. That time, I had been on Ritalin and even spent six months on lithium on top of that Ritalin, all to manage my "hyperkinesis", now known as ADHD. I didn't understand much about the daily pills at that time, but I knew my parents made me see Dr. Smith regularly: More so than other kids saw their pediatrician. I also knew that I didn't like him very much.

Dennis responded to my mom with some comforting statement but her response, which began as maternal concern, turned into anger and frustration. "He is so difficult and the meds don't seem to be helping!" Dennis mumbled something but she grew inconsolable in her diatribe. "Doctor Smith even said Leigh will probably end up dead or in jail by the time he's eighteen. And I'm starting to believe it!" My spy radar shot through the roof. I couldn't believe my luck! I was getting this all on tape! At this point, I didn't think much about what she had just said. In fact, I don't even know if the words sunk in at all. I was just so proud of my stealthy abilities that I retreated back to the safety of my room completely confident I was the next Maxwell Smart.

Half an hour later I heard the apartment door open and close as my mother bid farewell to Dennis. As I was calculating how I would get my tape recorder back if she decided to return to the living room, my mother flung open my bedroom door. The look of disgust on her face was one I had unfortunately grown used to. I lowered my eyes and saw through the haze of my dimly lit room that she held my tape recorder by its handle in her right hand. As a torrent of loud, angry words came streaming out of her mouth, I concentrated on nothing except the tape recorder she gripped tightly in her hand. It was no longer recording. I wondered how much I had taped before she stopped it. In the world of an intergalactic spy, as long as I'd gotten the information and escaped danger, I was a success. I couldn't wait to get my recorder back from her and listen to it under my sheets when she had gone to bed. I sat mute, waiting for her chastising to be over, eyes fixed on my machine. But she didn't just go away. Slowly, she placed my tape recorder down on my bureau and ejected the tape. Slowly, her right fingers pinched the exposed plastic tape at the bottom. Then she violently began pulling the tape from its casing. She pulled and pulled, wrapping the extra around her right hand in swirls of glistening brown as I sat on my bed willing the tears to stay away. She unraveled all of my hard work, along with the theme song to Doctor Who and my intergalactic super spy dreams.

Her deed done, my mother stormed out and slammed the door behind her. I hadn't heard her frustrated cries. I didn't know if she planned to punish me further. I did not care. My spying career was over, and her words finally rang in my ears:

"Dead or in jail by the time he's eighteen."

CHAPTER SEVEN

DON'T GET ALL HUFFY

It is common for people with ADHD to engage in thrill-seeking behavior. Initially, the assumption was that the impulsivity aspect of the disorder is what leads to this type of recklessness. In 1996, however, pharmacologist Kenneth Blum noted a specific chromosome sequence in DNA that led people with this sequence to have difficulty finding pleasure. These people have 20-30% fewer D2 dopamine receptors than the general population ("Reward Deficiency Syndrome"). Lacking dopamine results in an under stimulated pleasure portion of the brain. Consequently, in order for those with ADHD to feel really good, they have to do more of whatever it is that makes most people feel really good. This phenomena is knows as Reward Deficiency Syndrome (RDS). It is most commonly researched in conjunction with addictions such as alcoholism, gambling, over-eating, shopping, or sex. The science indicates that in order for someone with RDS to experience the same thrill as someone without this chromosomal sequence, they have to engage in a pleasure-inducing activity in excess.

Reward Deficiency Syndrome is often found in people with ADHD. For us, it might manifest in an addiction since we are prone to addictive behaviors, but it also may surface as thrill-seeking. Someone with RDS will only feel satisfied if they have taken something to the extreme. Jumping into a pond for a swim might be "fun", but for someone with RDS to get the same amount of "fun", he or she would need to cliff dive instead. Extreme sports and the gravitation towards other things associated with fearlessness may not actually be fearlessness, but rather RDS at work.

My wife frequently hears complaints from parents about their ADHD children who do not respond to discipline through the use of a reward system. This is one of the more frustrating aspects of RDS as demonstrated by younger children. Essentially, the child does not get enough pleasure out of the proposed reward (a sticker, marble, money…) to make him stop or deter them from a certain behavior. The old parenting trick of bribing your child to do something may not work at all on someone with RDS because there is more pleasure in the negative behavior than there is in the reward.

Renee's suggestion in these scenarios is to change the reward. It isn't that these children don't want to feel pleasure, it's that they need something more to experience it. Obviously you can't take your seven-year old sky-diving if they clean their room, but think about things that you *can* do that would be stimulating to that child. Conversely, you need to make whatever incorrect thing they may be doing into something that they do not find rewarding or stimulating. If they only receive attention when they are misbehaving, chances are they will continue misbehaving. They may possibly even misbehave more or to a greater extent, because that will feed their dopamine receptors more than behaving. My own childhood was full of situations where doing something wrong was far more interesting to me than doing something right.

And that's just wrong.

To be an adolescent boy in the early 1980s meant to own a BMX or Huffy bicycle. My family did not have a lot of money for luxuries or name-brands, but my parents did realize the importance of certain rites of passage for young men. When I turned eleven, I was given my very first new bike, a gorgeous Huffy Pro-Thunder that would quickly and easily become my most prized possession. Everyone who was anyone had one of those bikes and I was anxious to finally become like everyone else. I felt certain that having what other boys had would help me be accepted by my peers as a "normal"—or even cool kid.

I would ride my new bike every day after school. As I trolled the streets of our neighborhood I looked closely at the tires of the parked cars I passed. I searched to find chrome caps for the tire air gages that I could steal and put on the end of the pump valve for my Huffy. These chrome valve stem caps were all part of the cool-kid look that I desired. The boys in the neighborhood were always looking for them. If they already had two, they would look for two newer, shinier, fatter, thicker ones. Not only did those chrome caps look cool, they also proved that you had the balls to pluck them off of an automobile. The new, tricked out appearance of your bike was almost secondary to the fact that you had dared to break the law by taking something that wasn't yours.

I was no stranger to breaking the law so finding some chrome valve stem caps was easy for me, and soon my bike was a hot commodity. Perhaps I had made it a little too desirable because, one day, several months after I first got it, my treasured bicycle went missing. After cursing myself and my parents for not getting me a lock and chain, I chalked it up to yet another disappointment. The bike was gone, and the likelihood of getting it back was slim to none.

A few weeks passed with no sign of my Huffy. Then, one afternoon while I sat on my front porch, I spotted two boys riding down the street on a bike. One boy peddled and the other sat on the handlebars laughing wildly as the peddler increased his speed and wobbled a bit from the extra uneven weight. They were reveling in that joy of bike-ownership that I had only experienced for a brief period of time, but I as I looked closer, I knew that this wasn't bike ownership: it was robbery. That bike was *my* bike. It had been modified. There was new reflector tape on the body and some sort of shifter had been hooked up. It was scratched and slightly beat up, but I knew it was my Huffy. On the back bar where the strip of medal covered the back wheel, I had put my own reflector tape in two racing stripes running the length of the tire-cover. From my porch, I could see pieces of those reflector tape stripes that still remained, even after the little thieves had tried to peel off the rest.

I leapt up from my spot on the porch and ran just in front of the bike's path. The peddling boy slammed on the brakes and the boy on the handlebars slid off, landing on his feet, and swore quietly. The kid who had been steering got off but clutched onto the left handlebar protectively. I grabbed the other side of the handlebar and yanked the bike closer to me. "This is my bike! You stole my bike!" I yelled. I gave the handlebar another tug and brought the bike to my side. "You're not going anywhere! Give me back my bike." The boys looked shocked but simply stared at me. They didn't dispute my claims. They simply stood side-by-side, taking me in and glancing over my shoulder at the house in front of which I had been sitting. I didn't know what they were going to do. I didn't think about anything other than the strong, gut-wrenching desire to reclaim my dear Huffy bicycle and go back to my attempts to blend in with the cool crowd.

"Dad!" I beckoned for my father who had recently come home from work. "Dad! Dad!" I cried again. The boys continued to stare silently. My dad emerged from the house quickly. "It's my bike. They stole my bike!" I yelled to him as he made his way to the street. My father examined the faces of the two boys and the Huffy at my side.

"Are you sure it's your bike?" He asked me. I could

feel my head tilt to one side as if I was a dog who had heard a high-pitched whistle.

"Yes, dad. It's my bike," I insisted. My eyes looked up at him, angry and pleading. I could sense his inner struggle. His shoulders dropped. He tried to plaster on a polite smile and he put his hand on my shoulder.

"We can't really be sure of that." He said slowly. "Sorry boys. Here you go." And he placed his hand alongside my hand on *my* bike and wheeled it closer to the bullies. They didn't need to be told again. They grabbed my bike, spun it in the other direction, and hopped on, peddling furiously until they were soon disappearing down the street. It was my turn to stand in shock. "Come on inside," my father told me, and walked back to the house.

I knew that we lived in a rough part of town. Our area was made up of a mix of working class families and gangs. It was impossible to know if the boys who stole my bike were part of a gang, but I bet that this is what he was thinking. In his mind it was better to just let the bike go than risk the trouble that could follow when the boys told their family members that we had taken it back. We didn't know if taking that bike back meant taking a beating, or even worse. In hindsight, I know my father did the right thing. If he had been as certain as I was that the bike had been mine or if he had known that we would be safe afterwards, he may have behaved differently. I didn't understand this at the time.

In my eleven year old mind, these boys were just bullies regardless of their age, race, or socio-economic class. There was no distinction between those boys and the ones that taunted me and called me names at my elementary school. There was no distinction between those boys and the doctors and psychologists who told me that I couldn't or wouldn't amount to anything. There was no distinction between those boys and the people who viewed my ADHD as a disability that defined and hindered me. Giving in to them meant giving in to all of the bullies. Right or wrong, I was angry and hurt that my own father wouldn't stand up to them for me. I felt helpless and very much alone.

Although I lost my bike forever that day, I did gain a valuable lesson. There were people in my life that would try to protect me because they genuinely loved and cared about me. However, even though they had my best interests at heart, there was no guarantee that those people would be able to shut down the bullies that I would face in my future years. I would have to do this alone. The Huffy incident would sculpt how I would handle adversity from then on. It was the reason I did not seek help from my parents, teachers, doctors, or even from medication once I was old enough to refuse it for myself. If my future meant that I'd have to confront bully after bully, then I would face them, but I would tackle them alone and I would train my brain and body to take the negative and turn it into a positive. I would not be a product of a diagnosis and a world that viewed my condition as a hindrance. I would be a fighter. And I would have to take a lot of punches.

CHAPTER EIGHT

HERE COMES SPAZ

[Leigh] is now 91/2 years old, and is finishing up the 4th grade...Leigh continues to take the Ritalin 10mgs. twice a day morning and noon. There are no complaints of side effects...He seems rather "spacey" today...Leigh offers an interesting bit of history, reporting that he has had times when it appeared to him that everything in the surround was moving at an abnormal rate of speed. These episodes are not associated with alterations in consciousness or outward appearance changes...The episodic nature of his apparent school difficulty and the reports of sensory distortions raise the question of whether cerebral dysrhythmia may be a factor...We have decided to increase the morning does of Ritalin to 20 mgs. (Doctor's report April, 25, 1984)

When I started Ritalin, I was five years old. At the time the doctor wrote that "Because of the finding of significant distractibility and hyperactivity, we have begun Leigh on a clinical trial of stimulant medication" (Doctor's report August 15, 1979).

If you are a parent taking your child to a pediatrician, I highly suggest that you stay away from terms like "clinical trial". This is a red flag. Due to the results of my clinical trial, Ritalin now has several warnings, "In the presence of seizures, the drug should be discontinued" ("Ritalin"). I'm glad that my experiences can help other people, but, as a child, I was not appreciative of the experiments performed on my body. My doctor was a well-respected pediatric neurologist. We thought we were getting the best care possible. At the time, with the lack of knowledge out there on ADHD, maybe we were receiving the best care possible. In retrospect, however, I now know that a doctor that saw seizure activity once Ritalin was administered should have ceased the use of Ritalin altogether—never mind increasing the dosage!

If you're struggling with how to treat your or your child's ADHD, I strongly urge you to visit the CHADD (Children and Adults with ADHD) website and do a search for ADHD professionals ("CHADD"). Better yet, familiarize yourself with the possible warning signs of adverse effects to medication or behavioral therapy. No one knows you (or your child) better than you, so read up on the various doctors and options presented to you. There is nothing that says that you *need* to treat ADHD. There is no right way to treat ADHD.

But there is a wrong way.

Our rental home was conveniently close to my elementary school. By my fourth grade year, I was walking to and from school by myself. One day, I plotted along my regular route towards the back entrance of my school. As I approached the back of the school yard, I saw Jack. Jack was in elementary school but I think he already had a five o'clock shadow. Our city was not an affluent one and the student body of the surrounding schools reflected the struggles of the working middle-class families who lived there. Despite the fact that most of the children at the school maintained the same socioeconomic status, there was still an unspoken hierarchy among them. Like most unfortunate school dynamics the "popular" kids ruled and the outcasts were mercilessly teased. I was not popular and Jack and I were certainly not friends.

Jack and five of his cronies were loitering outside near the back door. I knew that I would have to walk by them in order to get inside. They spotted me as I entered the gated school yard. I could hear their murmurs starting and it wasn't long before they were purposefully audible enough for me to understand them clearly,

"Here comes Spaz. Look! Here he comes," they said. This nickname and mockery were not new to me. In fact, the name calling happened on a regular basis. "Spaz" was a favorite of the bullies. The fact that I was periodically having seizures certainly did nothing to dispel it. To their credit, the fourth graders were pretty clever with their insults. "I want a milkshake. Here, hold my milk, Spaz."

But Jack and his friends weren't there to merely mock me. They were bored, looking for something to do, and operating in the safety of a gang mentality. I slowed my pace. I imagined that there was an invisible force field around the half-dozen boys. Perhaps if I went a little bit to my right, they would shift a little to their left, and we would pass by like two enemy ships warily approaching one another on the sea. Instead, they drifted closer to me.

"Where ya going, Spaz?" one of the faceless minions asked. I didn't reply. I tried one last time to walk around their pack, but they shifted again, continuing to block the door to the school. Jack stepped away from the crowd and approached me. He was just barely taller than I was, but his dominance over me was obvious. We were almost toe to toe when he took his hands and placed his four fingertips just above my eyebrows. Before I had a chance to react, he pulled his hands down, raking his fingernails over my eyes and then my cheeks. It felt as if he'd tried to tear my eyes out. The pain was sharp and the air stung my exposed face but I did not have time to cry or put my hands to my cheeks because he started punching me.

He wasn't a skilled fighter, but he hit every part of me that he could find exposed. My backpack put me at a gross disadvantage. It began to slip off my left shoulder, rendering my left arm useless and my body horribly off-balance. Jack's gang watched from the sidelines, cheering on their leader. As he continued to kick and throw punches as me, I backed up without realizing it. At the back of the school was a black metal fire escape that led up to the third floor. I thought if I could get to the stairs, I could race up and escape the horrible beating. I got to the first step but couldn't turn myself all the way around to climb effectively because Jack was on my heels. I stumbled up to the first level, walking up backwards while Jack followed me, mercilessly and tirelessly swinging his arms and legs at me. I made it to the first landing and was able to wriggle out of my backpack; I dropped it there and continued to back up one, two, then three more steps. Jack stopped following me, but he picked up my backpack and began to twirl it in the air.

I used this moment to sneak down towards him on the landing. I don't know if I was going to hit him or run past him but I knew I needed to do something. I didn't get the chance. Swinging his arm like a softball pitcher, with my bag as the ball, Jack went around three times and then released the backpack as a perfect strike right into my face. The velocity of the backpack and the shock of it knocking into me jarred me off balance and I went tumbling down the rest of the stairs to the ground. I felt a sharp pain as my head made a dull thud against the cement of the play yard. For a second everything in my sight went bright and then black. Then, my sight was restored and I was aware not only of the pain on the left side of my head, but also that I was laying, helpless, in front of Jack's gang of lackeys. They had grown in number. School was starting shortly, and more students had arrived and were drawn to the crowd and noise in the

back of the yard. Maybe a dozen students coldly watched me writhe on the ground.

The blow to my head caused a soft ringing in the back of my eardrums. Blood trickled down my neck from a fresh scrape on my chin. I could still hear the boys around me laughing but it was muffled, as if I was underwater. As the ringing in my ears quieted, another sound emerged.

"Spaz! Spaz! Spaz! Spaz!…" The crowd of voices chanted together like a choir. "Spaz! Spaz! Spaz!…" And then, "Do it! Do it! Do it!" There was no time for bravery. Finally, I gave in and let the tears come. Through the water in my eyes, I saw my enemy. Jack stood over me, smirking down at his handiwork. He bent closer to me, cleared his throat, and released a wad of spit towards my head. It landed on my right hand, which was feebly trying to block my face and head, and slid down onto my cheek. He laughed and stood up, wound up again, and smashed my bag into my chest.

Mercifully, the school bell finally rang. The school day was starting, but my day had ended the moment I stepped foot onto the school yard. I thought I was saved by the bell as the majority of the crowd began to disperse, but then I felt hands grabbing me. Five thugs lifted me off of the cement, started walking towards the open dumpster, and tried to force me inside. With every last bit of strength I had, I grabbed at the padlock, the sides, the door hook, anything I could get my hands on so I could hold my body out of the garbage. It was to no avail. They tossed me in and closed the door. I heard a soft click and then a clang followed by laughter that grew softer and softer as they ran away into the school.

The stench was awful. Immediately, I reached for the side door they had pushed me through and tried to pull it open. It was padlocked. Defeated, I finally let the tears flow. "Why? Why had they done this to me?" I thought. These were questions that I would ask myself over and over again throughout my childhood, yet they would never be fully answered. I wanted to stay in that dumpster for the rest of the day and just dissolve into the fetid garbage that I felt that I was. How easy would it have been to just lay down and will the day away?

That wasn't who I was though. While I feared the repercussions I would face if I did not go to school, I also knew that the next beating would be worse if I showed Jack and his friends that they had gotten the best of me. Obviously, they'd won the physical fight, but I would be damned if I let them win over me mentally. I had to get out and I had to get to class. The opening at the top was up high, but this was when the lack of emptying the dumpster worked in my favor. I moved a couple of bags over to one side along the wall and used them as steps. Jumping up off the bags, I was able to get my chest onto the top of the opening and swing my right leg over it. From there, I shimmied the rest of my badly beaten out and then dropped down to the ground from the top of the dumpster.

By that time, everyone else was already inside the school. I retrieved my discarded backpack and went up the steps into the back of the building. The halls were empty. Looking down over my body, I saw various wet spots on my pants from grease, discarded drinks, or perhaps the school lunch's mystery-flavored Jell-O. I couldn't hide the stains, the dried blood, or the growing red spots that would turn into bruises on various parts of my body. But I could hide something. My shame.

I straightened my backpack on my shoulders, thrust them back, and began walking down the hall to my homeroom. Heads turned and strained to look outside of classroom doors as they heard my shuffling feet. I could hear faint muffled laughter from the onlookers, and then, as if to further drive a stake into my heart, I heard some faceless voice say loud and clear, "There's Spaz." *Yes*, I thought, *yes, here I am. And I'm not going away.* I reached my classroom and walked in as if it were any other day.

I think time stopped because no one moved for at least three seconds. Everyone, including my teacher, froze and stared at me as I slid into my assigned seat. I simply sat and looked ahead, nodding "hello" to my classmates as if I were not beaten to a pulp and covered in garbage. My teacher cleared her throat and turned her back to the class to resume writing the day's lesson on the chalkboard, and the normal buzz of a normal day started up once again.

I realized then that what my outside reflected: a beaten, dirty, worthless, "Spaz", did not have to be what was on my inside. And while it would take me years to fully understand how to prove that to the world, that day I proved it to the person who needed to know it the most.

Myself.

CHAPTER NINE

OH NO! JUDO

The H in ADHD can manifest in many different ways. One very common way is for it to cause impulsivity, which can be anything from blurting out something inappropriate to binge eating. There are so many aspects of life that are affected by one's lack of impulse control. For the most part, impulsivity occurs because the brain of someone with ADHD has not learned to pause and ponder over something before reacting. This inability to filter can have many negative connotations, but it can also be seen as creative and honest. When an ADHD mind is bored, irritated, or impatient, the tendency to be impulsive increases greatly. Perhaps this is because the ADHD mind loathes being bored so much that it decides to create its own entertainment.

It is important for those with ADHD to learn to "pause and ponder". If possible, they should write down the issue, question, idea, answer that pops into their head first and then re-read it to determine the best way to respond. This may be why something like a food journal can work to help curb impulsive eating. Being aware of what one is ingesting allows one to properly process whether or not it is worth ingesting at all.

Another useful way to thwart impulsivity is by doing things that require practicing mindfulness. An activity such as yoga can be good for ADHDers to learn, especially if they can implement that serene yoga breathing into their lives. If they can pause and breath before acting they will be less likely to perform impulsively.

I am not much of a yoga guy, but I did do something else that can be useful when trying to build impulse control. I took up martial arts. The strict discipline and dedication to this helped me more than I could have ever thought possible.

By the age of ten, I had settled into a life of Ritalin, Tegretal, and disappointment. I was not failing in school but I wasn't exactly a great student either. At home, I was still a "problem child" but I was somehow deemed old enough to go off and explore the streets on my own so I found myself under my parents' roof less and less. They placed their hopes and dreams in the future of my younger brother, who seemed to have luckily escaped the ADHD gene and was living a "normal" and "successful" childhood.

I spent many of my afternoons at the Boys' and Girls' Club. The club was conveniently open from 2:00-6:00pm Monday-Friday, which meant I could go right after school and stay until it was time to head home for dinner. My parents thought going there was a great idea because it kept me out of trouble and hopefully got some of my excess energy out.

One fateful day, I was waiting for the transport bus to take me to a nearby indoor pool. I was not especially good at swimming, and I still wore a back float even at age ten. This could have been mildly embarrassing, but just about everything about me was, so I didn't mind. As per usual my mind and body began to wander when the bus was taking too long to arrive. Clutching my towel and torpedo floatation device, I found myself following the sound of loud, aggressive yelling. It wasn't the type of yelling that signified a fight. It was a quick, abrupt, purposeful yell; A strong sound that was both intriguing and intimidating to me.

I followed the noise to a small, dingy room. In the middle of the room was a dirty-looking red, fold-out mat, and on that mat were several boys my age and older. At first glance, it looked like a street brawl. Boys were literally throwing one another over their shoulders. But then I realized that once one boy threw the other, he stepped back, allowed the boy on the floor to stand up, and then the thrower graciously became the throwee. There were five pairs of kids doing this repeatedly. With each throw came the roar of satisfaction that I had heard and followed to this new world. The boys wore stiff-looking white pants and a matching white jacket that was belted closed over their shirtless bodies. Off to the side stood the only grown-up in the room. He looked to be about forty. He was balding slightly and had a paunch of a belly that protruded slightly over his belt. He wore the same white pants and jacket as the kids in the room. He nodded approvingly in the direction of this pair and then that pair. Although his arms were crossed in front of him and his face looked stern, I could tell that he was encouraging the boys and they, in turn, threw each other harder and harder each time. I stood meekly at the doorway for less than a minute before I knew that I had to be a part of whatever was going on.

I decided to go back the next day in the hopes that I would catch the group in action again. I didn't plan to tell my parents. I didn't think they would look favorably on something that involved manhandling other children. They were afraid that I could easily become physically violent if pushed the wrong way. I did not have any inclination that this would happen, but I had been in trouble for outbursts at school. In truth, I did bite a girl once when I was in second, but in my mind she definitely deserved it.

Unbeknownst to me, my family, and possibly even my doctor at the time, aggressive behavior can be part of an ADHD diagnosis. It isn't that an ADHD person *wants* to hurt someone else. It's the impulsivity side of the disorder emerging. When a certain tingling, grinding sensation overwhelmed me, I had to elevate that sensation and the only way to do so was to act out. I felt strongly that joining this class, or whatever it was, would be life-changing. Although I didn't recognize it at the time, the ability to harness my excess energy *and* learn to beat people up was exactly what my ADHD mind needed.

I entered the room before the class started. I nervously approached the instructor. "Uh. Hi. My name is Leigh and I want to do this."

His face remained stoic. "This? You mean Judo?" Judo. I had heard of it but I didn't know what it was or what it would involve.

"Yes. Judo. I want to do Judo."

"All right. Leigh you said? You'll have to sign this form and you'll need $30 for the gi." I stared at him blankly. "The gi. It's the uniform, see?" He gestured to the two-piece white outfits that the others had on. My heart sank. I knew that I didn't have the money to buy the uniform. If I asked my parents for that amount they would never give it to me. It was not in our budget. We still lived in a cramped apartment and every penny my working-class family earned was put towards moving us out of there and into our own home. I lowered my eyes so the instructor wouldn't see my shame.

"I don't have that, Sir." I told him more politely than I had ever spoken to anyone before. I expected to be asked to leave or, at best, be told to sit down and watch, but I never expected what happened next. The instructor reached out and placed his hand on my shoulder. Despite his aged puffiness and gruff exterior, I saw something in his eyes that I had not seen much of in my brief ten years of life: kindness.

"Leigh, do you know what Judo means? It means 'gentle way', but don't let that fool you. There's nothing gentle about how we train. Now if you think you can handle it, I think there's an old gi around here somewhere that you could use. What do you say?"

What this man and I did not know then but what I know now is that his simple gesture would change the course of my life forever. Through Marital Arts I would learn to channel my frustrations. I would learn to respect others and to be respected in return. I would learn to hyperfocus on something productive and healthy. I would learn *to* focus on something for a sustained amount of time. The "gentle way" would show me a way to navigate through life's challenges that I would never forget. What else could I say?

"Yes! Oh thank you! Thank you! Yes!"

CHAPTER TEN

WHEN BAD DAYS HAPPEN TO BAD BOYS

Author Chris Ziegler Dendy states that "Succeeding in school is one of the most therapeutic things that can happen to a child." I could not agree more, but does the opposite apply as well? Is failing in school one of the most ego-torturing/mentally denigrating things that can happen to a child? Unfortunately, I have to conclude that it is. I never did succeed in school and, while that wore on me as a young adult trying to make it on my own in college, I believe that being unsuccessful socially was more difficult for me in my younger years.

There are many reasons why ADHD can create barriers to making and keeping friends. The most obvious is in the name, Attention Deficit *Hyperactive* Disorder. Hyperactivity that manifests in impulsivity can lead to explosive outbursts or to a bluntness that looks anti-social and rude and, consequently, tends to turn people off.

If this was the only "negative" aspect of ADHD, then it could be overlooked by people who are willing to make a go at a friendship, but there are many other attributes of ADHD that make it a bit of a challenge. ADHDers struggle to pay attention to the little things that matter to others, we may be argumentative, we believe there is only one way to do something, we can be overly sensitive, we are impatient, we don't learn from our mistakes, we can hyperfocus on the oddest things, we struggle to read social cues, we have no sense of time, we might be constantly fidgety or in motion physically or mentally, and we can easily become overwhelmed, anxious, depressed, angry, or sad. Being a young child with ADHD often means that you are a young child with few to no friends.

This type of social "failure" in school can certainly lead to academic failure in school as well. On the other hand, some children, especially inattentive children, may not even realize or care that he or she does not have many friends. One of the most important things my wife asks the clients who come to her deeply saddened by the fact that their child doesn't seem to have friends is, "Does that make your child upset?" All too often, the parent will respond with an emphatic "no". "Then," Renee tells them, "Don't let it make you upset."

However, stereotypically hyperactive children might thrive on social interactions and friendships. If this is the case, it becomes extremely detrimental to their social successes when they seem to be alone on an island. I didn't realize that friendships could carry such weight in our lives until I stepped back and remembered what it was like when I didn't have any.

It was a miserable, rainy afternoon in the spring of 1985. I was an awkward twelve-year-old sixth grader just trying to make it through the school year. It hadn't been a good day. I trudged home slowly, splashing through the puddles, in no hurry to get back to my apartment. I was bringing home a note from my teacher. Unfortunately, it wasn't a good note, but then again, I've never gotten a good note.

I had been talkative, or rowdy, or not paying attention in sixth grade math, and my teacher wanted to make sure my parents were aware of my poor choices and bad behavior. I knew the note would not be well-received, but that it had to be signed and returned the next day. It wasn't a death sentence, but it might mean that I couldn't watch *Star Trek* or *Doctor Who* that week—which may as well have been a death sentence.

I don't remember having the seizure. I blacked out. I can't articulate how or why I suddenly seized, but apparently, as I was walking home, I had a grand mal seizure. Someone was kind enough to stop and help me, and if not for that mystery Samaritan, I would have died. I would have died. I had fallen face down into a puddle and I remained there, seizing, but otherwise unable to move or get my head out of the puddle. Whoever saw me and called the ambulance saved me from drowning that day, and I am eternally grateful.

The next memory I have is waking up in the hospital emergency room. I was in a bed, wearing only one of those yellow hospital half-gowns tied around my neck. At twelve, the idea that anyone had seen me naked was more than embarrassing. In fact, the shame of my nudity far outweighed the shame of having to be carried into the ER for something that happened on a fairly regular basis.

As I came out of the fog that follows the end of every seizure, I began to assess the situation I was in. I was not in a private room. Instead, I had a drawn curtain on either side of my tiny hospital bed. I did not see my parents anywhere so I started to plan my escape. Just then, a doctor came in. He was not familiar, which was saying something. I'd seen a lot of doctors. He was middle aged, non-descript, and seemingly unconcerned with me as a patient.

"Well, Leigh," he began, "I wonder if you're ready to be straight with me now?" I stared at him blankly. "You see," he said as he sat on the edge of the twin bed, "We had to go through your backpack to identify you since you were brought in off the street." I got the sense that he was waiting for me to respond but I didn't know what he wanted me to say, so I nodded slightly. "Leigh. Leigh, we've seen the note." My brain, foggy and scared, tried to piece together what he was saying, but I still didn't quite get it. "We know you got in trouble at school today," he continued gently, but with an edge of annoyance. "We understand that you may have been nervous to go home today. So, Leigh, you know, if you pretended to have a seizure, you can just tell us…"

Suddenly, I had a moment of clarity and in that moment, I felt a rage growing inside me. Suddenly, the frustration of my school day, my seizures, my whole life, spilled out in an uncontrollable torrent of expletives. "Fuck you! Fuck you! Fuck this! Fuck you, man!" I screamed, as I leapt out of the bed. He didn't try to stop me, and I managed to pull back the curtains and head towards the waiting room. My legs were wobbly as I scrambled to get down the hallway. It wasn't until I opened the double doors to the waiting room that I realized my hospital gown had turned around, hinging on my neck and now flying like some sort of sad yellow superhero's cape behind my back. As I entered the crowded waiting room, I heard a voice, as sweet as a music box,

"Leigh? Leigh is that you?" I turned as I realized that I knew that sing-songy voice well. I locked eyes with Harriet, the dashing darling of my middle school. Her eyes widened in horror as she looked at me. I tried to smile, but then I followed her stare down, down, down, all way to my naked package. Her mom grabbed her head and turned it away. I saw that her thumb was wrapped in a cloth filled with ice and later learned that she had broken it at the same moment I was seizing on my walk home.

I looked away from her. To my right was a wall of mirrors, lined with pay phones. My brain began to truly wake as I saw what she had seen; a demented, twelve-year-old, naked Superman trying to escape the hospital. Immediately I grabbed a phonebook and tugged it over my groin area. I knew my best bet was to go back to my room, find my clothes, and then hide for the rest of my adolescence. I grinned an embarrassed smile and

started to dart back towards the double doors. I did not realize that the phone book was attached by a cord to the payphone station. The force with which I ran holding the phonebook recoiled when it came to the end of the cord. The phonebook tugged me viciously back towards the mirrored wall while I clung desperately to it. My balance failed me and I fell forwards, into the closed double doors. Without my hands to break my fall, my nose made the first contact with the doors and I tumbled to the floor where I remained, naked and bleeding, until a nurse came to hoist me up and take me back to my bed.

After that, I skipped school for four days. It wasn't that I was hurt or because I was recovering from my seizure. It was the complete and utter embarrassment that I felt. I knew I would see Harriet there. I had lusted after her every day of my sixth grade year. I would have to face her every day from then on, knowing that she had the image of my pubescent, naked body engrained in her head. Not only was I the dorky ADHD kid with a crush on her, but now I was Naked Super Seizure Man. And I had no super powers.

CHAPTER ELEVEN

GENERAL HOSPITAL

Many people have asked me about how I was able to cope with all the challenges I have dealt with throughout my life. That's an interesting question because I don't know if I have been able to cope the way the average, everyday person copes. According to <u>dictionary.com</u> "cope" means "to face and deal with responsibilities, problems, or difficulties, especially successfully or in a calm or adequate manner" ("Cope"). While most people would face and deal with their problems and then strive to get past them, I initially ignored them. Additionally, I would not say that I have always successfully, calmly, or adequately dealt with these adversities. Instead, I looked for ways to over-achieve and somewhat circumvent my problems. I felt that, if I over-achieved in some capacity, it would hide the pit falls of my "issues". I never realized that burying these things wasn't exactly healthy. But, over-achieving and using my laser focus on achieving certain tasks helped me "cope" with my ADHD in a way that I never expected.

If you pee in a glass and add enough water to it, you could dilute it enough to be fooled into drinking it. So I guess you could say that my life turned into a metaphorical glass of urine. I just kept adding water to it to hide the fact that there was any pee in there. You know when you go to a public pool full of people you don't know on a hot summer's day? You know, full well, that someone in this bunch of strangers has peed in the pool. Yet, you somehow convince yourself, maybe because the water is still blue, or because everyone else is doing it, or because it's just too dang hot outside, that it's OK to jump in. Once you're in the pool, you seem to forget about the fact that you were concerned with pee in the first place. You enjoy your swim.

In a way, this is sort of how I have managed my life. The bitter disappointments, the mistakes, the hardships, the daily struggle of my grinding brain, are the pee. My successes, my family, my hectic schedule, my joys, those are the water. If I can alter the ratio of pee to water, I can swim.

I spent my adult life focusing on what was possible rather than what was impossible. I can still hear the naysayers in my ear: "You can't do this", "You don't know what you're doing", "You're going to fail", "This is too hard for someone like you".

Someone like me.

Sure, I have failed more than I have succeeded. But I have tried more than I have given up. I have set my mind to accomplish more than what was laid out in front of me. Every time someone told me "you can't", I told myself "I can". I upped the amount of water in my glass. I cope with the pee, but the more water I add, the better my life will taste.

I was twelve when the alien abduction occurred. I was lifted out of my home and brought to a strange place where I was surrounded by white creatures who examined me for three days before they let me go. It was terrifying and confusing. The only solace I got came from the Voltron toy that I clung to throughout it all.

I was admitted to the hospital on a Tuesday in 1985 for three days of extensive testing and observation. It may as well have been an actual alien abduction because the experience was foreign and uncomfortable. Having been diagnosed with Hyperkinetic Disorder at the age of five, I was no stranger to doctors and tests, but this stint in the hospital was very different. Three weeks prior to my "capture," I experienced disorientation, loss of posture and unresponsiveness. My parents said that I was struggling with adjusting to my new sixth grade class. Upon release they described me as "violent and paranoid" to the doctors. This experience was supposed to answer questions about my diagnosis and give us all some hope. Instead, it only succeeded in scaring me.

My diagnosis upon arrival was Convulsive Disorder with Attention Deficit Disorder. I was an anomaly. The hospital had national acclaim and willingly accepted me as the perfect specimen and test subject, and I was abruptly "stolen" out of my home and brought to the hospital.

I was allowed to bring some comforts from home. My Voltron figurine was a logical choice. Voltron, the giant super robot that is formed from five pilot-driven space crafts, was a Transformer before its time. I was twelve years old and maybe I should have outgrown playing with dolls, but as a defender of the universe, he provided me with both safety and comfort in my strange surroundings.

After being checked in and led to a shared hospital room, the invasion truly began. The first thing I remember the aliens doing is taking my blood. I did not want to give up my precious blood so I resisted. I complained and yelled but the orderlies were large and overpowering. They were clearly interested in studying more than my blood, because I was poked and prodded from every angle. Voices and questions came from all sides. The doctors in front of me read my chart with "hmmmm"s and "ahhhhh"s as if they had any insight into my various "abnormalities". It was only the beginning.

I was led into a room that resembled a conference room. There, four "abductors" proceeded to bombard me with questions.

"How do you feel when you have a seizure?"

"What was the sequence of events that led up to the last seizure?"

"What happens when you have a seizure?"

I tried my best to answer them. The only way I could think to describe the feelings of an oncoming seizure was to say that it gave me a grinding feeling. It was a tingling, deep in the back of my throat and behind my eyes. Then my sense of depth would warp. My vision would focus and then unfocus. Finally, I'd black out and would have no recollection of the seizure or the events that followed it. They also asked me other questions too that didn't correlate with seizures. They had me draw a person and a clock and a random assortment of other things. I desperately wanted to get everything right, but I didn't know what "right" was. Were these the answers these creatures wanted? Was this enough information for them to "fix" me? I simply did not know. I just knew that Voltron and I were stuck there and that we were getting a great deal of attention at that hospital.

I was used to attention. I spent those first twelve years of my life receiving it, but this was different. The doctors and nurses that came to see me fussed over me. The women mothered me and made sure I was comfortable. One nurse even brought me extra dessert my second night. The doctors crowded me, talked to me, analyzed me, and made me feel like the most puzzling and interesting case they had ever seen. For once, I was not getting attention for being bad or for doing something wrong. Instead, I was getting attention because I was me. Leigh Macneil. Suddenly, "Spaz" was enormously important, and even when I was scared or anxious in that hospital, I was also a little bit proud.

The first day flew by. As night approached, it became clear that the "blood suckers" were not going to let me sleep much. I didn't know it at the time, but the nurses' task was to deprive me of sleep so I would sleep during my early morning EEG. I nodded off for an hour or so at a time, only to be awakened by someone coming to check my vitals, ask me questions, or even tell me that it was ok if I stayed up and watched the television long past my bedtime. Obviously, I took advantage of that option.

After dozing off briefly in the early morning hours, I heard a soft, sweet, unfamiliar voice say, "Leigh?" I opened my eyes hesitantly. Standing over me was a beautiful alien goddess. Her blond hair was pinned back in a sloppy bun and she had the kindest brown eyes I had ever seen. "Leigh, we have a busy day today. It's very early in the morning, but we have to get you ready for your EEG."

Shortly thereafter, I was made to lay down on a typical hospital table in a small room. Suddenly, my angelic nurse was gone and a faceless, unmemorable figure started explaining the process to me. Her hands worked quickly with a Q-tip and a squeeze bottle of some gelatinous liquid. She squirted the gel onto the Q-tip and then rubbed it aggressively into different places on my scalp. She worked quickly, sticking electrodes to each wet spot on my head. She stuck one on my ear. It tugged at my earlobe like a heavy earring. Once my head felt heavy from the amount of suction cup electrodes connected to wires on it, she lathered up my chin with the goo on a Q-tip. Pop. Electrode on my chin. Electrode on my eyelid. I certainly looked like an alien.

The nurse had me lay down carefully on the table and she adjusted the wires connected to the electrodes so that they were all behind me attached to a machine. She told me to relax and try to go to sleep as put a soft blanket over me and left the room, closing the door behind her.

And then the strobe light started.

I closed my eyes to try and block it out, but behind my eyelids I could see a kaleidoscope of bright flashes. The strobe flickered slowly. Then quickly. Then there were other lights that blinked off and on around the large, central strobe light. *How could anyone relax or fall asleep during this?* I thought. The weight on my head and the flashes of light above me were bothersome and uncomfortable but they did not cause a seizure. I laid there for what seemed like hours, not sleeping, not seizing, just willing it to be over. When it finally was, I was escorted back to my hospital room, where Voltron was waiting anxiously for my return and for the tales of what I had just experienced. The nurse that walked me back couldn't help but hide her disappointed look. I didn't realize that I had "failed" the EEG I hadn't given them a seizure.

What they did not know, and what I only realized later in life, is that I would not have had a seizure then because they had taken me off the Ritalin on Wednesday, five days before I began my hospital stay. The EEG administered on the second day of my abduction was a full six days off of the methylphenidate. This rendered me seizure-less. When I was discharged on the third day, I was dubbed "normal" and sent home to my parents to resume my regime of Tegretol and methylphenidate in the form of 20mg of Ritalin each morning. It was not long before the seizures started up again. They would continue until I weaned myself off the Ritalin. No one made the connection.

CHAPTER TWELVE

IF FOUND, PLEASE RETURN TO THE KITCHEN

Have you ever watched someone with ADHD doing something with such intense and complete focus that you assume their diagnosis is wrong? You think, "There's no way this person has ADHD because they are so immersed in what they are doing." You might see your child able to sit for an hour and create the most intricate Minecraft world imaginable, one that you can't even fathom how to build, yet he or she doesn't "understand" how to clean his or her room.

In our case, our older daughter can perform lengthy taekwondo routines that she has memorized while people walk all around her ring at a tournament. On the other hand, she could be told to go upstairs and brush her teeth, play with something that distracts her, and then realize she has no idea what she was doing up there in the first place.

So what is the difference? Why the paradox?

It all boils down to one thing—interest. If a person with ADHD is *interested* in something, they will focus on it intently, filter out distractions, set their mind to completing the task, and do it. The reason why it appears that their ADHD is gone is because, for whatever period of time they remain interested in the activity, their brains are able to function somewhat "normally". The science behind this in its simplest form is that the prefrontal cortex of the brain is engaged when interest peaks. This is the part of the brain that tends to be under-stimulated and in many cases even physically smaller in someone with ADHD. Therefore, when it is activated, it is able to focus and filter out distractions.

Conversely, if interest is not there, the traits of ADHD can be exacerbated and it can look like someone is having a flare-up of symptoms. We see this when we try to force our children to sit down and do homework or brush their teeth.

Even from a young age, I loved to work. I realize that I didn't always try or work in school, but that kind of work was mundane and pointless to me. I loved to work in a way that was productive, in a way that showed me a goal that I could then strive to achieve. School did no such thing. A good report card at the end of eight weeks was hardly something that I considered a goal or a sign of a productive mind. I needed something stimulating that would never be considered repetitive or monotonous. Little did I know that I would start my path to success at the tender age of thirteen in the most unlikely of places, a 24/7 chain restaurant.

My mother was working the third shift as a waitress at a restaurant. Third shift meant that she worked from 11:00pm-7:00am. She would sleep during the day while my eleven-year-old brother and I were at school. It was not a glamorous job, but it was a necessary one, and I am grateful that my mother recognized the need to do something to bring in money for the family while she went back to school. We struggled financially but my father worked hard during the day and my mother worked hard during the night.

One Saturday morning, around 3:00am, our home phone rang. It was my mother calling from work. She told my dad to wake me and my brother up. Apparently the dishwasher had not shown up and the manager, Sharon, said that desperate times called for desperate measures. Her call came right around the time that the restaurant experienced the most business. It was the only place that was open 24 hours and served breakfast food in that area, so this joint catered to the late-night/early-morning partiers, the trouble-makers, the dregs of society, and the people who worked night shifts. Between the hours of 3:00am-5:00am, the restaurant was swamped. So my brother and I were recruited to wash dishes. My brother cried and couldn't wait to go back home to bed, but I was filled with anticipation and excitement.

What I initially assumed would be a one-time gig ended up becoming a part-time job that I would grow to love. At age thirteen, you certainly aren't allowed to legally work at a chain restaurant establishment, especially third shift. Under normal circumstances, hiding my employment would have been easy, but the late-night crowd was prone to breaking out into drunken brawls. When that happened, the line cook would hide me in the walk-in cooler until the police had come and gone. I would hide there and then resurface once the coast was clear. That was how I spent my weekends for the next two years.

Although some may disapprove of this environment for a child, I found working there to be therapeutic. The exhilaration of the unknown and unexpected events of each night paired with my desire to keep the line clean of dishes kept my ADHD brain fully engaged, and I felt a sense of pride and accomplishment that I had never known before. The seeds were planted for the drive to succeed that has now become part of my daily life. I ached to move up in the restaurant's hierarchy.

There were three guys behind the line who customers could see through a rectangular cutout in the wall. Two of them cooked and one of them made the toast. I saw the toast-maker's spot as well within my grasp. Mostly, I just wanted to be seen from the front of the restaurant. I felt that this would represent a level of success, and I would be incredibly proud to be seen there. It would be my first promotion! The guy who currently made the toast was a drug dealer. During his shifts, he would have the man who ran his drugs meet him in the back of the restaurant by the loading dock. I offered my services as his lookout. This move was strategic—whenever the toast-maker left to make his drug deal, I would get to work behind the line making the toast. I figured that the more I was seen from that window, the more the manager would learn that I could be trusted with the all-important job assignment. It was the first time I wormed my way up the ladder of success in a thoroughly unconventional way, but it would not be the last.

CHAPTER THIRTEEN

WINNER TAKES ALL

"Children with ADHD wish to present a more positive view of themselves to others than is realistic in an effort to be more liked and positively evaluated by others, and out of fear of admitting they are not as good as they believe they ought to be" (Barkley 93). According to Dr. Barkley, children with ADHD will surround themselves with well-behaved, "star" children. This is something I did and I have found that I continue to do in my adult life. However, for a sensitive ADHD child, this can backfire in many ways.

Low self-esteem is a common trait among people with ADHD. It isn't necessarily due to a brain function, or lack thereof, but it is more a product of continually being told that they "can't" do something, or that they are "wrong" or "bad". These judgements or past experiences can often lead the child to believe that they really "can't", or that they are actually "bad". This can lead to serious self-doubt. ADHD kids will second-guess themselves. They will believe that they can't, so they won't.

On the other end of the spectrum is something that I see in my own daughter—something that she, no doubt, inherited from me. Isabelle has a false sense of her abilities. This is known as Positive Illusory Bias, or PIB. One definition of PIB says that it "refers to a person's report of higher self-esteem than is warranted by his or her behavior...[an] exaggeration of one's competence" ("Home"). Isabelle will always volunteer to go first to demonstrate something, even when she hasn't fully learned or mastered the task. I've also seen her practice something once and then heard her say the dreaded "I got it", when, in fact she doesn't "have it" at all.

While researching ADHD, Renee and I noticed that Positive Illusory Bias is often referred to as an undesirable trait to possess. There are various strategies to "fix" this condition. We, however, disagree with this assessment. If I think I can do something, I will do it. When Isabelle volunteers or attempts something that she thinks she can do, and she fails, I do not see her crumple and become disheartened in this failure. Why not? Because I don't call it a failure. Her mother and I are her biggest cheerleaders. Renee and I treat everything she attempts to do as a success, simply because she has attempted something at all. If you don't try, you will never do.

When you don't have people behind you as your cheerleaders, you must be your own.

Just because I was branded a loser didn't mean that I wanted to be a loser. Towards the end of my high school career, I realized that if I surrounded myself with "winners", then maybe some of their star power would rub off on me. In my mind, the "nerds" were winners because they were having success in school, something that I could never do. I saw that their futures were laid out like red carpets in front of them. I wasn't your typical kid who saw the popular jocks as the "winners". Those with the top GPAs were the real successes. I knew that those were the kids that had the drive and ambition that I so desperately wanted. I knew that their hard-work was going to take them places, and I wanted to go places as well! I was fortunate that my science fiction-loving side enabled me to be welcomed into friendships with the so-called "nerds" and that is where I learned about success.

It was our common affection for *Dungeons and Dragons*, *Doctor Who*, *Star Trek*, and role-playing games that brought me and the "nerds" together. Our Friday and Saturday nights would be spent in basements on Bulletin Boards (BBS Boards), playing games rather than going out to parties with the rest of our classmates. Those guys accepted me despite all of my faults. They were the people who treated me as their equal, even though I had been told all of my life that I was anything but. They did not make fun of my grades, my ADHD, or my seizures like most of the other students at my high school; instead they welcomed and embraced me and realized that my quirkiness was just a cool part of me.

I quickly figured out that not only did I enjoy their company, but I enjoyed the way their company made me feel. They were *smart* and I thought that if I could surround myself with smart, successful people, then I could be smart and successful too—or at least look like I was. I tried to emulate their behaviors. I saw them study and I watched them complete book reports, science reports, projects, etc.... and I thought, "that's what I need to do!" So, I would start. And then I would stop. I would try to study and then I would procrastinate. I would do what they did. And I would fail.

The most difficult thing for people to understand about me as a student with ADHD is that, I *wanted* to study. I *wanted* to do my homework. I *wanted* to be a "nerd". It became extremely frustrating for me because I would sit down and read two or three pages of something and then I would lose interest. I would wait an hour and go back and read two or three more pages and then I would lose focus again. By the time I went back to the reading a third time, I'd forget what happened the first two times I read. I just could not read and comprehend something on my own. I had no context for what I was reading. My brain didn't understand what I was supposed to absorb from the assignments.

If given physical or visual instruction, however, I could do just about anything. I could learn in science class if we were shown an experiment and then asked to replicate it. I could learn jujitsu by watching the instructor and then trying the moves. I could even learn math if someone did a problem on the board in front of me and then let me try to work out a similar problem. However, if I just read something, or if I just had to sit there and be lectured, I could not learn it. I watched in envy as my smart friends climbed their way up the class ranks, stepping on one another's heads along the way. Although I knew I was not like them, I thought maybe I could fool others into thinking that I was.

All that really mattered was that I fooled myself. As I struggled through my low-level classes, I kept convincing myself that I was going to be a "winner". I was going to be a winner in a world that constantly called me a loser. I would show the world that winners come in all different forms and that winners are made, not born—through hard-work, determination, and a little bit of *Dungeons and Dragons*

CHAPTER FOURTEEN

WRESTLEMANIA

ADHD is often known for its many paradoxical traits. It is certainly a blessing and a curse. One of the most fascinating paradoxes is how ADHD causes distractibility but can also cause hyperfocus. Those who have experience with hyperfocus know all too well how it can quickly take over and become all-consuming. It's hard to step out of my own head to explain hyperfocus because I don't see it from the outside when I am doing it. When Renee gives workshops, she often uses me as an example, and this area is no different.

In 2014, a large-scale Ebola outbreak occurred, starting in West Africa. From there, cases were spread to the United States and caused deaths on U.S. soil. Like anyone else, I watched the news for more details, but then I began to hyperfocus and obsess about the outbreak. Before long, I had stock-piled our food and water storage and devised an escape plan from any and all nearby cities should we need it. I listened to talk radio constantly. I stayed alert for updates. I was vigilant. I called this being prepared. It seemed smart and logical.

This hyperfocus can be "contagious" to others with ADHD—especially children. During the time of the Ebola scare, my intense hyper-focus caused our then six-year-old daughter, Isabelle, to hyperfocus as well. We did not know the extent to which it consumed her mind until the school emailed Renee to tell her that Isabelle, while sitting next to another child who happened to sneeze, turned to that child and immediately asked him if he had Ebola. Isabelle would come home and ask for updates on the outbreak. She was fully able to discuss the path that the virus had followed to get here into the United States and who it had infected and affected. Needless to say, the rest of the kindergarteners were not impressed with Isabelle's Ebola knowledge and the fear she seemed to carry along with that knowledge. Her teacher was not impressed either.

Can hyperfocus be beneficial? Sure, if it is directed properly. It can certainly benefit an adult in their work, but they must be able to identify that they *are* hyperfocusing, and be able to tear themselves away from whatever it is that holds their attention so thoroughly. If you ask Renee now, she will tell you that I hyperfocus on pinball. In the last several months, we have purchased three pinball machines, I have gone to a pinball expo, I have gotten on a first name basis with a local arcade owner, and I have YouTube videos of pinball bookmarked on our television. Is this a negative in our lives? Not at all. As long as I don't let it take over my life. Besides, pinball is a lot of fun!

When I began wrestling, I discovered that learning how to do it was just as challenging as learning how to do schoolwork. I wanted to learn quickly and I wanted to learn it all, but like with school, I had trouble listening and then applying a skill. Even at a young age, I realized that I learned differently, so I tried untraditional methods. I began watching videos in addition to going to seminars. I would watch video after video and then, during a two hour practice, I would try every move I had seen. My results were mediocre at best. I joked that I was the janitor's apprentice because I had been pinned so many times that I could tell him exactly which lights were out on the gym ceiling.

One day, during the middle of my high school wrestling practice, my coach pulled me aside and asked me a question that would stick with me my entire life. "Leigh!! Who do you want to be?" he yelled in my face. "A jack of all trades and master of none, or the master of one trade that can jack'em all? It's your choice!" He didn't wait for me to answer, which was wise because I hardly understood the question. Instead, he just walked away to tend to my other teammates. I stood there, awkwardly unsure of what I supposed to do then. I decided to pretend like I needed a water break and went to the cooler where I could sit for a minute. *What did I want to be?* I didn't know, but I did know what I didn't want to be: "Dead or in jail by the time he's eighteen."

At the time, my idol was recent Olympic wrestling gold medalist, John Smith. After a successful high school and college career, John Smith went on to be a four-time World Champion, two-time gold medalist, and a multi-championship winning coach of Oklahoma State University. He obviously had many skills, but he was known for his single-leg take-down. Though it was one of the most basic wrestling moves taught in clinics and teams throughout the world, no one could stop John Smith's single-leg take-down. His opponents all knew it was coming. They admitted to watching videos of Smith wrestling over and over again, trying to devise a plan for how they would be the one to take the title from him. They all failed.

John Smith had mastered this one move all the way to a gold medal. As I sat on the bench, thinking about what I wanted to be, I realized I hadn't mastered anything. I wasn't a good student. I wasn't a good wrestler. I wasn't a good son. I had let the naysayers into my head enough to convince me that I had to learn everything all at once in order to be successful. I thought the way to prove them wrong was to be just OK at *everything* instead of realizing that, if I could figure out how to be really good at one thing, my mind would begin to understand how to learn. Once I could learn, I could be a master. A master of what? That remained to be seen, but I was going to be good at something, and no one was going to stop me.

CHAPTER FIFTEEN

SEIZE THE DAY

To medicate or not to medicate? That is the question. What is the answer? It's not a simple one. Choosing to use medication is a very personal decision. There are many factors involved.

Medications can be broken down into two categories. There are the stimulants: amphetamines, methamphetamines, and methylphenidate. The second category is the non-stimulants: atomoxetine (Strattera), clonidine (Kapvay), and guanfacine (Intuniv). Some people are intimidated by the term "stimulant" and wish to stay away from those types of medications. They are known for their adverse side-effects such as decreased appetite, difficulty sleeping, irritability, tics, and increased blood pressure. Contrary to popular belief however, non-stimulants also have side-effects. They just tend to be more unique and specific to each individual drug.

People always ask Renee about medication. "Which one should I try first?" "Which one do you recommend?"

"Do I need to medicate at all?". She is quick to say that there isn't one definitive answer. Medicating, like most other treatments for ADHD, is about trial and error. Although a doctor can suggest a drug based on the patient's most prevalent symptoms (hyperactivity, impulsivity, or distractibility), there is no guarantee that any given medication will be a good fit.

Nowadays there are companies who do genetic testing that will suggest which medications will be most likely to work with one's DNA. GeneSight and Harmonyx are two such companies. Their genetic testing and medication matching can be purchased and completed at your home and then mailed out to their labs for the results. If you're considering medicating for ADHD, it isn't a bad idea to try this as a first step in finding the right drug, but the results are not perfect.

In truth, we will never know what a medication will do to a person until he or she takes it. And sometimes, even when we are taking it, we don't recognize the side-effects for what they are. I am certainly living proof of that. When I was young there was really only one go-to medication for ADHD—Ritalin. I was put on Ritalin when I was five. Nowadays, it is not recommended for anyone under the age of six, but in 1979, no one realized its potentially harmful effect on very young children. The most recent research also states that "In the presence of seizures, the drug should be discontinued" ("Ritalin"). I often wonder what my life would have looked like if my parents and I had known a little bit more about Ritalin before I started taking it, but hindsight really *is* 20-20.

By the time I entered my first year of high school, everyone knew me as the kid who had seizures. At that point, I was having a petite mal or a grande mal seizure at least once a week. Needless to say, I was not a friend-magnet. The kids who tolerated me did so with wariness.

I was on the seizure medication Tegretal. It did not stop or even lesson the seizures. The fact that no one made the connection between the seizures and the Ritalin I was taking still astonishes me. By the time I was 9 ½, I had gone through three dose increases of Ritalin, with a little "side-vacation" also on lithium, which did not prove "successful". During my visit to Dr. Smith in 1984, I was described as "spacey". The doctor's solution was to increase my dose of Ritalin by 50%.

Eight months later, as these episodes grew more severe and more frequent, the doctor determined that I was experiencing "mild temporal lobe seizures despite a normal brain wave". I was put on the anticonvulsant, Tegretol, along with my daily dose of Ritalin. More drugs to treat the thing that the drugs were causing. My life continued, seizure after seizure, with no evidence of a brain disorder such as epilepsy. In fact, every neurologic exam came back perfectly normal, despite the fact that I was having regular seizures.

When I entered high school, things were looking very grim. began to be truly aware of the feelings in my body. I knew they weren't typical teenage sentiments. If I expressed them, I knew I would end up back in Dr. Smith's office on who knows what medication, but I could no longer ignore them. The sensations are hard to describe. To say "my skin felt like it was crawling" would be a cliché, and an understatement. I felt enormous anxiety about everything. I grew embarrassed of myself. I was basically en route to becoming the failure that everyone told me I would be. Academically, I was always in the lowest level classes. Socially, I was limited to the number of friends who would associate with me. At home, I was the problem child who would never amount to anything. The fear of being "dead or in jail by the age of eighteen" was no longer just a fear. It looked like it was going to become my reality.

As I grew more and more paranoid and stressed about every little thing, a thought that I did not want to acknowledge started to creep into my anxious brain. I contemplated suicide. It wasn't that I wanted to kill myself; I just didn't know how to live with myself.

I also could not ignore the unbridled cruelty of my fellow high schoolers. Kids are not kind, and they are even less kind to a teenager with seizures. I was ridiculed, mocked, and called every name in the book. Those that befriended me subjected themselves to teasing as well so I often attracted the kids who were already being teased for their own awkwardness. On the totem pole of coolness, a nerdy kid will always be up higher than a kid with seizures. This, plus the fact that I still identified as a science fiction junky, put me at the bottom of the "cool pole". It was lonely at the bottom.

I was looking for some release. Some freedom from the constant feeling that my life was joyless. I wanted to blame someone or something for making me feel the way I did. The obvious object of resentment was my pill bottles. I hated that I felt chained to them; that somehow, if I stopped using them to treat my seizures or my "mental disorder", I would feel much, much worse. I couldn't imagine what "worse" would be at that point. I was constantly depressed, always anxious, contemplating ending my life, and having seizures on a regular basis. Something in me finally woke up and said *I refuse to be that kid any longer.* I was tired of being a slave to the medications, so I did what seemed like the logical thing: I stopped taking them.

As a high school student in a society where most kids turned *to* drugs, I wanted to get as far away from them as possible.

I pretended to take my pills daily when, in actuality, I was throwing them away. As I slowly started to come off the meds, I noticed a change in my body. I began to see that I could focus on certain aspects of schooling. I knew that I still struggled academically, but I found an inner drive that I'd never known I had. Suddenly, I did not want to give in to the people who doubted my abilities. Suddenly, I was no longer resigned to being a failure. I was going to be a success, but I was going to have to do it on my own.

Off of the Ritalin, I found that the seizures went from one week apart to two weeks apart to one month apart. Eventually, they subsided altogether. No one could explain the "miraculous" vanishing of my neurological seizure disorder. Only I knew the truth.

At that time I was nearly a year away from being completely out of the house, which meant that I was still under my parents' care for medical purposes. I knew that they would never approve of my coming off of the Ritalin. So I knew I had to come up with a way to hide the fact that I was not taking my daily dose. I do not condone or endorse weaning yourself off of medication at all. It was a foolish and dangerous thing to do and I do not advise anyone else to take this route, but it is, unfortunately, the way I handled the situation. Despite its downfalls and medical endangerment to my health, I came off of my medication. I remained seizure-free.

At the age of eighteen, I not only became responsible for my own medical well-being, but I was also finally able to gain true independence. After a seizure free year, I was finally able to get my driver's license. That was the end of my childhood in so many ways. I was a new person, a new man, and I was going to start living for the first time in my life.

It was time to go to college.

CHAPTER SIXTEEN

THE OPPOSITE
OF DEATH

Although most children are diagnosed with ADHD sometime during elementary school, the American Academy of Pediatrics states that it is possible to diagnose kids as young as 4 years of age. This is not very common because it can be difficult to discern a typical toddler from one with ADHD. However, it is not impossible. When I was diagnosed in 1979, the term ADHD did not exist. Attention Deficit Disorder became the term for the diagnosis in 1980 and, later, in 1988, this disorder was dubbed Attention Deficit Hyperactive Disorder (with or without hyperactivity). Prior to that, people with ADHD were diagnosed with what I was diagnosed with: "Hyperkinetic Disorder".

Although the symptoms that go hand in hand with Hyperkinetic Disorder had existed and been studied for years, in 1979, recognizing it as a legitimate "illness" was still relatively new. At the time of my diagnosis, I don't think that my parents really cared what it was called, as long as I was labeled with something that could explain my erratic behavior. I don't believe anyone could have possibly foreseen the impact this early diagnosis would have on me not only as a young child, but also as an adult.

A study published on October 4, 2010 found that "Children with ADHD at 4 to 6 years of age were at greatly increased risk for meeting *DSM-IV* criteria for major depression…and for attempting suicide through the age of 18 years relative to comparison children" (Chronis-Tuscano). The logic behind this is simple: the earlier children are diagnosed, the longer they've been exposed to bullying, self-consciousness, self-loathing, etc. The impact that a negative upbringing has on them can culminate in such a lack of self-worth they can feel depressed and worthless enough to think that the world would be unaffected, or even better, if they were not in it. Suicide in the late teen years and early adult years is common because it is around that time that expectations for the future are made clear. These can present an enormous amount of pressure for any young adult, but especially for those with ADHD who already feel that they are not "enough".

The link between suicide and ADHD is still under-researched. While there is an obvious link between suicide attempts and people with ADHD, the actual *reason* behind this cannot be pinpointed. We know that many people with ADHD also have anxiety and/or depression, but we do not know if those conditions are the cause of their suicidal thoughts or feelings. The lack of scientific evidence leads me to believe that there is no actual scientific link, but rather, social and environmental links. It's difficult for someone who has been the butt of demeaning jokes and disappointment his whole life to believe that everything will turn out fine in the end. Instead, he might assume that there is nothing else to live for.

I can assure you, however, that there is everything to live for. It may take some time to figure out how your ADHD attributes can work in your favor, but I promise you that there is every reason to believe that you can turn all those negative things you were told in your youth into the fuel to motivate you in your future.

If you or someone you know is feeling especially down, don't be afraid to reach out for some help. The National Suicide Prevention Lifeline is available 24 hours a day by calling 1-800-273-8255. Remember, the world is a better place with you in it.

At eighteen my life was not going in the direction I wanted it to go. Although I had forgone the use of all medications and I was neither dead nor in jail yet, I'd hit a low point. A very, very low point.

School had always been challenging for me and senior year of high school proved to be no different. However, the stakes were higher. Not passing a required class senior year meant not graduating, and that was exactly where I was headed.

My psychology teacher was also the theater director at my high school. On top of the fact that psychology did not particularly interest me, she spent much of the class talking about what was going on in the theater department of our school, which was a topic that interested me even less. Her course was difficult for me to follow since her lessons were peppered with "theater talk", and as the end of the year approached, it became apparent that I was not going to pass psychology.

Because of this failure, I would not be able to graduate on time. I was told that I would be allowed to complete a psychology course in summer school and, if I passed that, I would be awarded my diploma. The bottom line was that I could not graduate, or even walk, with my classmates. It was the ultimate humiliation for me. I was already a year behind, having taken kindergarten twice. At this point, I was a year older than most of them and yet I would not be able to graduate with my fellow seniors.

This devastation dug deep into my core. Not only had I failed at something again, but I had failed in such a way that I could not blame anyone or anything else. I was not on Ritalin anymore, I was not influenced by my parents or their rules since I was an "adult", and I did not have any reason to avoid studying. I just could not do it. And because of my inability to work around my procrastination and my distractions, I was ashamed to admit that I would not graduate high school on time.

It was a dark time. Although I had been upset and let down before, it had never been to that degree. I could no longer ignore the negative self-talk that was creeping in. I hated myself. I began to have thoughts of suicide.

Some mornings I would drive to a park before school.

As a senior, I had the privilege of late arrival, so after everyone had gone to work or school, there was hardly ever anyone at the park by late morning. There I sat in the parking lot and listened to depressing Pearl Jam tunes, and I realized that my whole life could culminate in failure. Suicidal thoughts surged through my head. If my future was in fact dead or in jail, I chose dead. What was there to live for?

Yet somehow, I still pulled out of the parking spot each time and drove to school. After all of my rumination on death and failure, I discovered that I knew a way out of my depression. If my future was to fail, then I was already dead. But what if my future was to succeed? The same mantra that kept me down could be negated and lift me up. If my future was to succeed, then I was already alive.

I finished my senior year and enrolled in a summer school psychology class. With a different teacher and a lackadaisical summer school vibe, I was able to easily pass and earn my diploma. When it arrived in the mail, it may have been anti-climactic, but it did not make that diploma any less real. I was finally back on track. Even though I did not know where that path would lead, I knew I would not be to death. The only option, therefore, was to succeed.

CHAPTER SEVENTEEN

NINETEEN TO LIFE

Temper tantrums in young children are generally accepted as normal. The "terrible twos" for example, are legendary. However, for a child with ADHD, a build-up of emotion and the inability to regulate that emotion can look like a temper tantrum well into the elementary and possibly even middle school years. These outbursts can be misinterpreted. A teacher or parent might just think they have a "difficult" child and not realize that an outburst is caused by an aspect of that child's ADHD brain. Worse, other parents may judge the parenting of that child and assume that his or her parents aren't doing a good job, or that they spoil their child, or that they don't know how to discipline that child.

While not all outbursts can be attributed to ADHD, there are many reasons why a child with ADHD is more prone to have an outburst than a child without. Anger combined with impulsivity is very powerful. If this occurs, a young child can have a physical, visceral reaction. My oldest daughter was prone to this type of reaction when she was about four years old. Her go-to response when she was frustrated, upset, or angry, was to hit. It didn't matter that hitting was "wrong". It didn't matter that she would receive a punishment for this reaction. It didn't matter that she would lose playdates with friends whose moms just didn't understand. None of those things could stop her from the impulse to hit because she did not have the ability to pause, process, and then filter her reaction accordingly.

This type of response may adjust as a child ages. A thirteen-year-old is less likely to lash out with a physical slap and more likely to lash out with hurtful words, or destructive behavior (either to themselves or to their environment). An older child or adult with ADHD may have such a wall built around them after years of negative reinforcement, that they misinterpret signals and automatically go in attack mode.

The difference between an ADHDer who struggles with this type of emotional regulation and someone who may have some anger or other, deeper, issues, is that someone with ADHD does not act out of true anger. They will generally realize they have exploded and will quite quickly feel guilty or regretful. They will often not understand what caused them to have such a fiery response, but they may also struggle with how to prevent it from happening again.

I fully realize that my wife receives the brunt of my impulsive, negative outbursts. What she has learned to understand is that I'm generally not angry—simply frustrated or impatient. Unfortunately, those we care most about are the ones that experience all of the backlash. If you are lucky as I have been, you will find someone who will understand and be able to call you out on these reactions. I don't know if I will ever be able to fully squelch the feeling that builds up in me which causes me to have an outburst, but I do know that understanding my ADHD has been instrumental in creating harmony in my friendships and my family life.

I knew I had a purpose in life but my purpose was not to be where I was at nineteen-years-old. The naysayers continued to taunt me. Some of them were my own family and friends. They told me that I "should be happy." My parents insisted that graduating was "enough" and that I should be proud and satisfied that I had gotten that far. They were certainly impressed with me and that felt good. But it was not far enough, and I refused to settle. All of my high school friends were off to continue on their paths to success. They all settled into their years at elite schools and they were well on their way to doing great things.

I believe seeing their successes is partly what drove me to try for my own. It wasn't that I necessarily *wanted* to go to college, but I didn't want to live with the embarrassment of not going to college. I didn't want to hear "we told you so" or other such negative statements from people who did not believe in me. Therefore, once I earned my high school diploma, I knew that college would be the most logical next step and I knew that my belief in myself was the only thing I could rely on.

During the fall semester of 1992, I was living at home as I began taking night courses at a small college. I worked part-time at a supermarket and a retail store while I paid for two courses at this college. My hope was that the classes would rehabilitate my transcript and earn me the grades to prove to other schools that I was eligible to be a full-time student. My first choice of school had already issued me a rejection letter for the fall, so I thought I would start with a couple of classes locally and earn my way into it.

A few months into that semester I had what could have been a setback, but proved to be a life-changing motivator. My parents and I had a falling out. It is hard to say at this point who or what caused the disagreement, as we had many in those days, but that one was enough to force me out of the house. Had this not taken place, it would have been easy to become complacent and live rent-free indefinitely. That was not my path. Since most of my earnings were going towards tuition, I had to find an inexpensive solution to homelessness.

Luckily, my friend and co-worker, Derek, was willing to share his basement apartment with me. Honestly, it was more like a room. A friendly French-Canadian fellow named Pierre rented out three rooms in a nearby house, two upstairs, and one in the basement. We took the basement, which certainly had its limitations—including no bathroom. My part of the apartment consisted of a twin mattress on the floor in the corner, which I surrounded with banana cartons that contained my clothes. Derek was my age but was a reservist in the Marines so he worked at the local grocery store when he was home. Although I admired him, the military was not an option for me. I had already been rejected by them due to my past medical history and my flat feet, so college remained my goal.

Although living on my own was a dream of mine, doing so in a shared basement "apartment" was not part of the dream. Derek already planned to go to the college I wanted to go to the following fall and I had visions of myself back at the grocery store full-time unless I managed to earn acceptable grades in night school.

I took a sociology course and an English course, Introduction to Writing, that fall. I earned a D+ in sociology and a C in English. The grades themselves were somewhat devastating, but the reality that I was doing everything all on my own was inspiring. I had very little contact with my parents. They continued to question my motives for taking classes and did not think I would be able to handle college full-time. Their doubts only fueled my desire to make something of myself. When I applied to my desired college for the second time, I was rejected again. It could have been the end. But, of course, it wasn't.

CHAPTER EIGHTEEN

HOW I GOT INTO COLLEGE

I became an avid follower of Grant Cardone, author, entrepreneur, and training expert, a few years ago. Although he does not speak to ADHD directly, I found that many of his principles closely aligned with mine. Additionally, they certainly cater to the way my ADHD mind works. When addressing the topic of failure, Grant Cardone states, "Most people fail only because they are operating at the wrong degree of action. To simply action, we are going to break down your choices in four simple categories or degrees of action. Your four choices are: 1. Do nothing. 2. Retreat. 3. Take normal levels of action. 4. Take massive action" (Cardone 48). Once I read this, I realized that I spent almost my entire life operating on the fourth choice, "Take massive action."

Some of this action may have been accidental and impulsive, but some of it also came from determination and wanting to prove the negative people in my life wrong. Renee and I have come to see that, for every negative trait to ADHD, there can be a positive. You just have to change the way you look at things. Inattentiveness can spawn creativity. Hyperfocus creates diligence and attention to detail. Hyperactivity causes boundless amounts of energy. Impulsivity manifests as spontaneity. The list can go on and on. I would urge you to start your own list though. What are the traits caused by ADHD that you, your family, or friends struggle with the most? Write them down and then think about each one. Isn't there something good, even if it seems like a stretch for you to come up with, that can come from this trait?

This activity may be challenging. The truth is, ADHD is a legitimate disability and we would never want to discredit that. However, I am asking that you look for ways to make the most out of the way your brain works. We cannot change our hardwiring. We can medicate. We can get behavioral therapy. We can be coached. We can mature and learn acceptable behavior. We can do any number of things to manage our ADHD, but the reality is, we were made this way and these things are merely tools in the toolbox that is our body. The best things you can do for yourself or your child, friend, or spouse with ADHD is to figure out your strengths. The rest of the world will tell you your weaknesses over and over again. You need a stockpile of strengths on tap to refute that negativity.

The ADHD community is truly divided on how to handle and discuss both the challenging and the redeeming aspects of the disorder. An article on the website The Activist Post by Eric Blair stirred up attention with its title: "Is ADHD an evolutionary gift in a rapidly changing world?". In this article he suggested that ADHD could be the way brains are adapting to the new technologically advanced world. Conversely, Dr. Russell Barkley, a well-known authority on ADHD, made a shocking statement at the 2009 CADDAC Conference. In his lecture he said, "ADHD is no gift. There is no evidence in any research on any of hundreds of measures that we have taken that show that ADHD predisposes to anything positive in human life" (Barkley). Dr. Barkley has done much for the advancement of ADHA and, while his talk initially seems degrading, I can see where he is coming from. His argument attempts to uphold ADHD as a disability protected under section 504. Resources and support for the disorder have come a long way since I was a boy and it would be devastating for society to regress. And, let's face it, having ADHD is hard and we have earned the title "disability." Both ends of the spectrum take it to the extreme. It's a shame if people feel that they have to choose a side when both "sides" could actually exist simultaneously.

When discussing his commitment to "Take massive action", Grant Cardone said, "I have been called a lot of things due to my commitment to action—a workaholic, obsessive, greedy, never satisfied, driven, and even manic" (Cardone 57). I just want Grant to know that he is not alone. I am determined to achieve my goals in this way 100% and 100% of the time. Whether that is a positive or a negative aspect of my ADHD is irrelevant to me.

I choose to look at it as *my* strength. And I choose to believe that I have many more.

I suppose that, after nineteen years, I would have expected and accepted rejection rather well, but I was no longer going to be that kid. I was a new man—one that would get into college despite having received a second rejection letter. I did the most reasonable thing my brain could think of; I looked at the name of the admissions employee that signed my rejection letter and I set out to find him. The next day, I drove myself to the college campus. I followed the campus signs that read "Admissions" and I parked my car. I sauntered up to the secretary of the Admission's Office and informed her that it was imperative that I speak with the man in charge. To this day, I'm not really sure what I said or did to convince her that she should allow me to go talk to this man, but she did.

I was in my nicest khakis and pale blue button-down shirt. I tried to be poised and refined, but neither of those things are my strong point. I pulled out my rejection letter and the transcripts I had from my college courses.

"Look, I just got my rejection letter. I know that I haven't had a good track record in high school or in this first semester of night classes, but I want a chance." I think I saw his ears perk up so I continued, "I want to do the work. I am dedicated to the work. I am going to do what it takes to do the work." He looked like he was ready to interject with another rejection so I just continued, babbling rapidly, "I had a hard life growing up. I had to take medication to help me get through school, but that still didn't work. I had seizures and everyone made fun of me. I need you to give me a chance. I need another shot." I continued rambling. I feared that, if he was given the chance to speak, he would run me out of his office. He would call in his nice secretary and she would see me to the door and then I would be back where I was before, in a spiral of self-loathing and self-doubt with no hope of crawling out of that hole in the near future. I told that man every pathetic thing I could think of. It sounded like a sob story, but it was *my* story. I concluded with, "I drove all the way up here just to find you to beg you to please just give me a shot and let me be a student here."

There was silence. A lot of silence. Finally he said, "You know, you do not meet our school's basic academic requirements" I lowered my eyes "However, I am impressed that you came here and found me to talk to me. Are you truly committed to doing the work?" I had lost a bit of my confidence by that point. My answer, albeit soft-spoken, was an emphatic,

"Yes sir." The "man in charge" told me that he would consider what we'd discussed and then quickly dismissed me from his office. I did not argue or try to convince him any further. I took the discipline that I had learned through my years of judo and the martial arts and realized that, if I wanted to earn someone's respect, I had to demonstrate that I was worthy of it. I think I nearly bowed when I left the office with my fate in his hands.

I returned to my normal routine of waiting tables

and stocking the vegetables. A week passed before I received something from the college in the mail. It was an acceptance letter. I was invited to start school in the second semester. I had no idea how I was going to pay for tuition, where I would live, or how I could succeed in full-time school at the university level, but I was going to try.

Naysayers beware!

CHAPTER NINETEEN

FINALLY FINITE

Because the ADHD mind is different than the mind of someone without ADHD, it is no surprise that someone with ADHD will learn differently than a "normal" person. One of the reasons why so many young ADHD students struggle, or even fail, is because they haven't been allowed to discover how they learn most effectively.

There are at least seven different types of learning styles. Visual (spatial), aural (auditory), verbal (lingusistic), kinesthetic (physical), logical (mathematical), social (interpersonal), and solitary (intrapersonal). Most people learn best through one or two of these styles, but many people, especially students in elementary and middle school, do not know which of these works best for them. If a student's learning style is not identified and explored, it becomes a true challenge for that student to learn easily.

For example, if a student has ADHD with physical hyperactivity, he or she might be a kinesthetic learner. This learner might learn best if he or she is able to move around during a lesson or while information is taught or processed by that student. What might this look like in action? Again, it is unique to each person, but it could mean reading textbooks while on a stationary bike, bouncing on an exercise ball in class rather than at a regular chair at the desk, fidgeting with a spinner/cube/necklace/pencil topper that is sold for this purpose, etc. My wife goes for long runs to enable ideas to develop.

Allowing people to discover and then utilize their learning styles will allow them to have incredible success, both inside of the classroom and out in the work force.

When your life has been spent hearing that college is not in your future, especially when you think you might not even have a future, you find that you are a little bit lost when you do actually end up in college. By the age of nineteen, I had worked my way into a university and, for the first time in my life, I was focused on finding academic triumph in the classroom.

I did not know what to major in because I did not know what interested me. No one had ever asked me what I wanted to be or do with my life so I had not given it much thought. I chose to major in accounting by default. My dad was an accountant and I thought perhaps I had inherited some interest in numbers from him. In order to major in accounting, however, I had to take a course called "Finite Math". This class was known to be challenging for even the best pupils because the professor relied on the students' ability to read several chapters before a class and then to come in knowing the content. I had class on Tuesday and Thursday mornings.

One Tuesday when I entered the classroom, the professor had several equations written on the board. The equations were in Row Echelon form. I understood enough from the previous chapters to recognize that. But I didn't know anything else about the equations. I had sat down to read my Finite Math chapters numerous times over the previous weekend. Every time I tried to read, I just could not grasp the concepts being introduced. I would read for two hours and not know or understand a thing about what I had just read. I'd take a break and then return to the chapters, from the start again, and it was as if I had never seen the words before.

Prior to the professor's demonstration of the problems on the board, we had a ten-question quiz at the start of the class. The problems on the quiz were the same ones written on the board. They appeared just as foreign to me on the paper in front of me as they had on the board when I entered the room. The quiz was meant to assess the knowledge we'd gained through the reading prior to class. I got eight problems wrong on the quiz. I sat there with my 20% glaring at me, reminding me of the failure that I had been promised my whole life and wondering if college had really been the impossibility that I'd been told it would be. However, once the professor began to do the problems on the board, I realized something.

I understood them.

I knew how to solve them. After the professor's visual demonstration, I knew exactly what to do and how to do it. The Row Echelon form grew clear in my head and I saw how to break down the problems and find their answers. When it came time for us to take the exam that covered the items on the previous quizzes, I aced the test. Not only that, but I received extra credit for being one of the first people finished. I had found success in the most unlikely of places—in school.

Of course, my final grade for the course was not impressive. My frequent and numerous failing quiz grades far outnumbered the amount of passing exam grades I had in the books, but I felt that I had earned more than just a C+ in the class. I had gained an understanding of how I learned best. Suddenly, everything seemed clear. I learned differently than other students, and that was perfectly okay.

CHAPTER TWENTY

THE BEST LAID PLANS...

Attention Deficit is often synonymous with distractibility. Most of the people diagnosed with ADHD struggle with staying focused and on task, and we blame this on distractibility. This isn't entirely accurate. The truth is, people with ADHD tend to pay close attention to lots of things and this is what causes distractibility. There is an inability to filter what is important and what is not. The ADHD brain thinks everything is important. In his book, *Healing ADD,* Doctor Daniel Amen describes the cause of distractibility to be "hypersensitivity to the environment", and states that "People with ADD, however, are often hypersensitive to their senses, and they have trouble suppressing the sounds, sights, smells, and feel of the environment—the sensory noise that surrounds us" (Amen 23-24). In other words, the world distracts us because we pay attention to everything in it all at once. This mental restlessness is one version of hyperactivity that can manifest in someone with ADHD.

Environmental stimuli is not the only thing that can

cause the brain to struggle with focus. Internal stimuli can also be distracting. If the brain cannot escape constant rumination or the sensation that it is racing, it is impossible to focus on any given task. Challenges can also arise when a person is hypersensitive to things associated with the five senses. The ADHDer's negative reaction to how something tastes, sounds, feels, etc., can result in an inability to pay attention to whatever it is he or she should be paying attention to. This hypersensitivity can be the cause of many sensory issues that seem to overlap with ADHD. For instance, my oldest daughter can't stand to have buttons on her pants or tags in her clothes. She is nine years old and has yet to wear a pair of jeans because she can't handle the waistband-buttons-zipper combination. Our youngest strongly dislikes light, gentle touches. Everything about her is strong and aggressive. If you try to softly tickle her arm, she recoils angrily. She would rather you rubbed or scratched her with hard pressure. These sensitivities are quite common in people with ADHD.

These hypersensitivities to one or more of the five senses can help us understand attention issues. In *Healing ADD*, Doctor Amen discusses the sensitivity to sight as being problematic:

> In a similar way, sight sensitivity is a frequent problem...When driving, for example, it is important to focus on the road. Many people with ADD, however, see everything around them, becoming

> bombarded with visual stimuli. Reading a book also requires you to block out extraneous visual stimuli. Unfortunately, many people with ADD are unable to do this and they are frequently distracted by the movements around them. (Amen 25)

Attention challenges plague everyone with ADHD, but it is the cause of the distraction that will differ from person to person. Because of this, we need different tactics to keep distractions at bay. Strategies like wearing headphones or ear plugs, listening to white noise, keeping a memo pad handy for when something comes to your mind, using fidget tools while focusing on something else, and scheduling uninterrupted blocks of time can be effective. Of course everything is trial and error. One may have to try several strategies before finding something that works.

I know my mind constantly feels like it is racing. Sometimes is it virtually impossible for me to slow it down, enjoy myself, and live in the moment. I don't enjoy vacationing because I can't force stillness upon my brain, whereas Renee can enjoy a cocktail and the beach for hours. After a lifetime with this brain, however, I have learned to accept certain things and to adapt accordingly. In my down time, I try to listen to auto books or do something else that will quiet the mind. Renee often tells her clients that I can simultaneously watch TV, listen to talk radio, and reply to an email, yet be completely unable to answer a question coherently while doing any one of these things in isolation.

Rather than worry about the things that will take your mind away from its desired focus, why not worry about finding the things that your mind focuses on all on its own. What keeps you interested? What do you find stimulating? Knowing the answers to questions like these can be especially beneficial as you try to find a successful career path. If you choose a path where your job is constantly changing, shifting, bringing new challenges, and requires you to be a go-getter, then you may find success in that field, like I did. Stick with that. Don't think you have to conform to a desk job or a cubicle. I would go absolutely insane if I had to spend my days in an office. And while I say that I don't like to travel for my job, I'm sure the change of location, pace, and day-to-day schedule is part of what makes me good at it. It is all about finding your niche.

I may have had the desire and the motivation to do the work as a full-time student in college, but I did not always have the ability. While I was finding success with the unconventional way my Finite Math professor taught, I struggled in other classes that were more traditional. The standard lecture with notes, reading, and studying had not worked as an instructional technique for me in high school, and it certainly was not effective in college. Despite the knowledge that I had to learn, process, and study differently than others, I still thought I could succeed if I maintained that I was just like everybody else.

One Sunday night my five rambunctious roommates were socializing and enjoying themselves as usual. They were all locals to the area and had hordes of mutual friends. Our apartment was often the starting point for several guys to rally and meet up before a night out. While I got along with all of them and they accepted me into their tight-knit group, it was clear that I was different. I did not really enjoying drinking to excess. As a twenty-year old full-time student who also had to work constantly, I had little time for extra-curricular imbibing. I also knew how hard I had worked to simply be there in college, and I did not want to jeopardize my presence there or waste my time doing anything that would prevent me from making something of myself. So while my roommates planned to drink their evening away, I had different ideas.

I knew I had several chapters to read for a Managerial Accounting class the next day. It was five o'clock and I felt certain that I had plenty of time to get everything done. I mentally prepared myself to start the reading right then. I hunkered down in my room but could still hear the rowdy cheers from the living room where my roommates watched football. I looked at the time again: 5:03. I figured they would be gone shortly because they would want to grab a slice of pizza or something before heading out for the night. My book was opened on my bed, calling to me, but I felt that I would probably retain the information a lot better if I waited for them to leave.

I set my alarm for 6:30pm and went out into the living room.

In what seemed like no time at all, the alarm went off and beckoned me back to my chapters. I was resolved to finish. I said goodnight to my roommates who were about to leave and shut myself back into my bedroom.

Sprawled across my bed laying on my stomach, I propped my textbook up by my pillow and rested my chin on my hands. I read one page. I had no idea what it said. I went back a paragraph. Then two paragraphs. I re-read the whole page. I started feeling tired. Maybe I needed a nap to focus? I set my alarm for 8:30pm and allowed the sleep to take over.

The buzzing alarm pierced through my dreams. I got up groggily, went to the bathroom, and then returned to my place on my bed, ready to study. I tried starting on the second page of my reading. I knew I was reading with my eyes, but very little of it seemed to be sinking in. I willed myself to pay attention, and then my stomach let out a loud grumble.

"Hey! I haven't eaten dinner," I said out loud. Obviously I would not be able to study on an empty stomach. It was 8:52pm. I set my alarm for 9:30 that night. A quick bite should be all I needed to get going again. By the time I'd finished eating a quick sandwich, I could hear my alarm screaming away. I went back into my room and took my book off the bed. This time I would take it out to the living room for a change of scenery. My roommates would be out for another few hours, and I

would easily be able to finish what I had left to read in that time.

Page three. The material was boring and tedious, but that time I made it through several pages. I didn't really know exactly what I was supposed to grasp from the assignment, but I felt certain that I wasn't doing it right. I heard a sound at the front door. It was two of my roommates, a little wobbly on their feet, returning for the night. "Called it a night, huh?" I asked. They said they were and went to bed. By that point, I was completely distracted. I resigned myself to the fact that there would be no more reading for the night. I set my alarm for 4:00am and went to bed.

4:00am. Still dark outside. I had a better plan. I would get up around 8:00am and head to the coffee shop down the street where I could finish my chapters before my 10:00am class. The comforting thoughts of that new and excellent plan lulled me back to sleep.

When I woke up I had every intention of following the plan. I got dressed, grabbed my book, shoved it into my backpack, and headed out the door. "Do I need money?" I asked myself. "Probably. I'd better stop." I began to walk in the direction of the ATM. "Where's my wallet? Shit!" I'd left it at home. I turned around and rushed into the house. The door was locked. Where were my keys? I knocked and knocked. One of my roommates groggily came to door and unlocked it. "Thanks!" I mumbled. I ran in and ransacked my room trying to remember where I'd put my wallet. "When did I have it last? Wait! Is it? It *is* in my backpack!" Back out the door I went. "ARGH!" I still needed to get cash.

It should not have been a surprise to me that I never did make it to the coffee shop to read my chapters, although I did have just enough time to get a cup of coffee and bring it with me to my Managerial Accounting class that Monday morning. The events of the previous night and the subsequent events that morning became par for the course. I always had the best intentions of getting my work done. I had the desire and the motivation to prove people wrong, to be a good student, to show that I could succeed, but I just could not follow through. My grades began to suffer and I saw my previous high school years about to be replayed in my college years. But I was *paying* to go to school—out of my own pocket. My parents, although they were proud of my decision, were not capable of helping me through college. Additionally, they didn't fully support my determination to go to school in the first place. They feared it would be too much of a struggle for me, a waste of time. I know they were trying to protect me from failure, but I saw their lack of support as just another obstacle to conquer. However, my inability to study made me wonder if my mother had been right when she'd said she feared that I was not physically capable of going to college, and I could feel my depression creeping in like a dark cloud before a thunderstorm.

I made the decision to go see a doctor. I didn't have health insurance at the time and I certainly couldn't afford the visit, but I felt like I also couldn't afford *not* to go. The visit was nothing monumental. We mostly spoke about my previous history with ADHD. I told him about the medications I was on as a child, when I went off them, and the symptoms I was experiencing now that caused me to be distracted and unable to buckle down with my classes, despite truly wanting to be a good student. The entire conversation may have lasted five minutes. Then he prescribed me some Ritalin and sent me on my way. I was tremendously nervous to resume taking Ritalin. I remembered that I didn't like how it made me feel when I was in elementary, middle, and high school. I did not know if it had truly helped me concentrate and keep my ADHD at bay or if it was merely something that the professionals thought would tame my "wild child" side. I might have tossed the prescription right into the trash had I not known other adults on Ritalin.

At the time, I was on the college wrestling team. I had earned my black belt in judo after several years with the Boys and Girls Club program and I had easily transitioned to wrestling in high school. Although I was probably the worst wrestler on the team, I was still on it, and I took great pride in that. Several of my fellow wrestlers took Ritalin and claimed that it helped them to focus. I was ready to start being a productive student, so I fulfilled my prescription for 20mg of Ritalin and hoped for the best.

I diligently took my Ritalin for the next few days. By day three, I started to feel anxious. My irritability skyrocketed. I began snapping at my roommates. Five days into the medication and my temper was out of control. I felt aggressive and angry. I got into a fight at a party. My teeth felt itchy. There was a bizarre ringing in my ears. In class and in my studies, I found I could focus a bit more, but the side effects were much worse than the benefits.

After I'd been fully medicated for ten days, I sat in the basement classroom of my Managerial Accounting class. People were chatting while the professor walked around and distributed papers. The class had yet to start. I collected my handouts and arranged my papers on the tiny desk top. It was one of those uncomfortable school desks where the desk top attached to the chair portion. They were far too small for most college students, but this school didn't seem to have the budget for improvements. Suddenly, I felt a familiar grinding sensation behind my eyes. My ears started buzzing and my eyes unfocused and then re-focused. I looked down at my right hand holding my pencil, and it was as if I couldn't keep my fingers around it. I saw the pencil drop and roll off the desk, but before it hit the ground, I blacked out entirely. When I came to, disoriented and confused, I was in a hospital bed with no recollection of how I'd gotten there.

I'd had a grand mal seizure. I was later told that it was especially violent and disturbing, and it resulted in a concussion. Had I been in elementary school, the teacher would have known about my seizures, cleared some space around me as I convulsed, called my parents, and sent me home for the day. In college, however, no one knew my seizure history. No one had ever put together that it was the Ritalin that had caused my seizures. My doctor and parents had maintained that I'd had epilepsy and had simply grown out of it. It had been nearly four years since my last seizure. I thought that I had escaped that part of my life when I escaped high school.

I was released from the hospital fairly quickly once I informed the doctor of my medical history. He, like the rest of the medical world before him, chalked my seizure up my supposed epilepsy, and I went on my way after promising that I would see my regular doctor for a follow up immediately (a promise that I had no intention of keeping). I thought I could return to my anonymous existence among the few thousand other students at the college. I was horribly wrong.

By the next day, it was apparent to me that my world had changed. My roommates uncomfortably welcomed me home with kind words, but they avoided eye contact and did not even give me the standard pat-on-the-back that men often exchanged in greeting. One of them who normally walked to school with me made an excuse and backed out. I believe he viewed me as a bomb that had a timer set to detonate. Therefore, I set out alone to walk the mile to my sociology class which was in the main building on campus. This hall sits in front of an outdoor green and commons area so it was always a hangout for students throughout the year. I approached the main campus on foot and, immediately, I could feel the sets of eyes on me.

This wasn't a large school; total enrollment in the 1990s was around 4,000. That day as I walked to sociology, I felt certain that I passed all 3,999 other students, and that they all knew what had happened to me in class the day before. Out of the corner of my eye, I saw people whispering. I could feel the stares from all sides. I was instantly uncomfortable, as if I was walking down the middle of the road naked. I was no longer Leigh Macneil, college student. I was "Spaz", "ADHD and seizure disorder boy" all over again. I was twenty years old and I was still that kid.

A few of the sociology students had also been in my accounting class the previous day. When I entered the room, a couple of them asked me if I was ok. I tried to laugh it off, "Oh yeah, yeah. I'm good," I replied nonchalantly, as if nothing significant had happened. But inside I felt that everything significant had happened. Perhaps it was all in my head, but I really believed that I was back to square one again.

A few days later, I had another seizure. It was a petite mal seizure and it happened in my bedroom. My roommates were present, which only made their wariness of me grow. After that episode, I decided to stop taking the Ritalin. I didn't know if I could pass my college courses without it, but I did know that I couldn't pass them feeling as defeated and as dejected as I felt after those seizures. I had to find a way to fight for myself. I was outed as "different" once again, and I could either let that break me or march on through the emotional pain and academic struggles. The way I saw it, there was only one choice.

CHAPTER TWENTY-ONE:

CAR SALES OR BUST

When someone first researches ADHD, they will encounter the term "executive function(ing)" quite a bit. Sheldon H. Horowitz, Ed.D explains, "It [executive functioning] requires the ability to analyze situations, plan and take action, focus and maintain attention, and adjust actions as needed to get the job done." If executive functioning is in charge of things like self-regulation, working memory, sustaining attention, organizing, and planning, it is easy to understand that so many aspects of your life can be affected by an impairment in these areas.

As people grow older, it generally becomes more obvious to them when they are struggling with executive functions, and they may in turn be able to adjust their mindset or behaviors accordingly. For children, however, this task is much more challenging. If parents of children with ADHD, can learn to look for signs that they are struggling in one area or another, perhaps they can start to make them aware of the reasoning behind their struggles. This awareness serves several purposes.

Let's say impulsivity is a common problem in a child. Imagine if we could teach the child a strategy to stop before performing an impulsive act and reflect on what is about to occur. Instilling this ability to pause is one of the most important things a person with ADHD can learn to do. Renee likens it to the "Easy" button, made popular by the Staples stores some years back. If kids could learn to push the "Pause" button before making impulsive decisions or acting out, think of the difference it could make!

I was introduced to the car business in 1995. There was no training or ceremonial rite involved. Instead, I was thrust onto the sales floor during the President's Day Weekend Sales Event at a well-known car dealership. This dealership looked like something straight out of a television show in the 1950's. Everyone there resembled Herb from "*WKRP in Cincinnati*". Those guys could sell cars, but I quickly realized that learning from them was not an option. They sat at their desks and waited for their repeat customers to walk in. The fact that most of them were nearing seventy meant that they had sold cars to the same people for decades. Folks walked in, found their polyester pants suited dealer, and they walked out with a car. If I was going to be successful in the business, I would have to do it on my own—as usual. But, I was determined that car sales would be my calling.

It wasn't so much that I wanted to be a car salesman. I just had a need to do *something*. Up until that point, I'd had two jobs. One was waiting tables and the other was at a youth detention center. The day an inmate tried to stab with me a hypodermic needle filled with his own HIV positive blood was the day I knew that my detention center days were over. I was faced with the real-life possibility of being a waiter for the rest of my life, and while that is a great option for some, it was not a great option for me. (Truthfully, I wasn't even very good at waiting tables, but I had a big smile and a look of desperation so my tips were generally pretty good.) When I was twenty-two, I met a guy at the gym who worked at a Volvo dealership, and I noticed that he seemed to drive a new car every other week. I figured if you got to drive new Volvos and you still had time to go to the gym and sport some man-jewelry, then car sales might not be a bad gig.

It was the mid-1990s and the country was coming out of a recession so finding dealerships that were looking for sales people was easy. I went in for interview after interview in my Dockers and my thin Oak Tree tie and, interview after interview, I was turned down. Everyone wanted someone with experience and I clearly did not have any. I was ready to give up and resign myself to the possibility of "dead or in jail by the age of eighteen", when I stumbled across an ad for a salesperson opening at a local car dealership. Something in my head told me that I needed to call. A gruff voice identifying itself as belonging to the general manager of the place answered the phone.

"Hello sir," I began, "I uh. I saw your ad in the paper. I just want to let you know that I don't have any experience and I have never sold a car before. The only thing I've ever sold is a bottle of wine. So far, nobody wants to talk to me so I don't want to waste your time, but is it worth me coming in and filling out an application?" There was a pause. In that moment that stretched on for eternity, I realized that I had just given this man the worst sales pitch of all time. The man on the other line cleared his throat.

"You know, selling cars is no different than selling a bottle of wine during a fancy meal; it's just on a bigger plate. See you when you get here."

And with that, I was in!

CHAPTER TWENTY-TWO:

LET'S MAKE A SALE

There is a phenomenon known as the Performance-Pressure Paradigm which is outlined in ADD Coach Academy courses. Essentially, it explains why people with ADHD struggle so much when they are put under pressure. When pressure begins to build, regardless of whether it is external pressure from parents or teachers or whether it is internal pressure from the individual him/herself, it can be incredibly overwhelming. This causes a decrease in performance and concentration, which leads to failure. Failure stimulates pressure once again until a cycle is formed. The more intense the deadline or the requirements, the less likely it is that the ADHDer will be able to complete it.

This may be one of the reasons why it appears that ADHDers procrastinate or perform poorly on tasks. Another possibility could be that he or she is afraid of doing something wrong, yet again. This is known as Perfection Paralysis. The fear of not being perfect is what hinders a person from initially attempting or starting something. If they are not sure that they can do something perfectly, then they are unable to try it for fear of this perceived failure.

ADHD will manifest in different people in different ways. Just as no two people are exactly alike, no two cases of ADHD are exactly alike. To believe that we fit into a "one-size-fits-all" mold is to negate so much of what this book is trying to teach. It is fair to say, however, that most if not all ADHDers have the perseverance to get something done, even if they lack the ability to see it through. So much of my determination to achieve a goal, and the creativity that I use to achieve that same goal, stems from my ADHD brain. Once I have my mind set, it is nearly impossible to deter or distract me from my mission. In this regard, the distractibility in Attention Deficit Hyperactive Disorder is virtually nonexistent, but there is a stubbornness and dedicated side to those with ADHD that is unparalleled.

As I settled in to being one of seven sales people at the respected car dealership, I quickly realized that I did not know anything about sales. While the other employees didn't offer to help me, I could still learn from them. I watched their interactions. I tried to pick up on their tactics. I greeted every customer that walked in the door. I smiled and shook countless hands, but I was not selling as many cars as I wanted.

I was determined to do whatever was necessary to be successful. I showed up to work early. I stayed late. I made friends with clients and my fellow salesmen. I was doing all right, but I wasn't making the type of impact that I desired. I certainly wasn't making the type of money I required to make ends meet. I needed to figure out how to make my mark and succeed in sales but I didn't know where to start until I spent some time at my friend Richard's house.

Ever since high school I'd known that I loved computers, but I was not smart or wealthy enough to be a real "computer geek". I did not know much about how they worked and I certainly didn't have the money to buy one. Fortunately, I had some legitimate computer geek friends like Richard.

On a cold winter day in November, I bribed Richard with some pizza to build me a computer. I had the parts and pieces, but I had no idea how they went together. Fortunately, Richard was a budding computer genius and he knew exactly what he was doing. As he tinkered away while I "helped," I talked to him about my dilemma at work. I felt sure that the key to success was to build relationships with my customers, but my scattered, multi-tasking brain struggled with intrapersonal relationships and I had trouble remembering the little things about each client. When I explained this to Richard, he said, "Well, why don't we create a program so you can keep track of your customers?"

Ding! Ding! Ding!

"Can we do that?" I asked incredulously.

"Yes. Absolutely. Do you have anything like that?"

"Nah. All I have is a pile of Purchase and Sales slips

and Up sheets. I tried doing what all of the other sales people do, which is to just have a rotating call schedule on random pieces of paper, but that doesn't work for me." I chucked at the recollection of my fellow sales people, in their 70's style plaid suits, aimlessly spinning their Rolladexes with sticky notes protruding from the tops and sides of the note cards.

"I'm surprised that works for anyone!" Richard scoffed. "What kinds of things do you want to keep track of?" I thought about it and he and I eventually came up with a list of everything trackable. This included: types of vehicles people were looking for but we didn't have in stock, addresses, phone numbers, trades, trade values, dates, birthdays, and anniversaries. Richard assured me that we could create a program to document all of these variables that even I could manage. So that's what we set out to do.

We used the most basic computer program to create what is now known as a CRM or Customer Relationship Manager. It's a way to track inventory and customers that, today, has become a big business. If Richard and I had been most astute at the time, we would have marketed our program and become millionaires. Alas, we only succeeded in making my life a little bit easier, but this program became my go-to. I used it religiously. All I had to do was enter data, and then it became searchable. If my manager went out and bought a car at auction, I could enter the car's make and model into my search field. Instantly, a list of people who were looking for that car would appear (if I had entered this information previously). It seems rudimentary now, but this was before people were using the Internet, and the fact that I could access this information by merely typing in a few words was a game changer for my life in sales.

The most frequent thing I used the CRM for was to honor celebrations in people's lives. I would go to the thrift store and buy birthday cards, Christmas cards, anniversary cards, Easter cards; anything I could find that would be a reason to celebrate. Then, with the information I had stored in my CRM, I would mail cards at appropriate times. I would write a little note "Looking forward to celebrating with you and a new car", "Did you get that new car you asked Santa for?" "Let me know if I can help make this year even better than the one before". I would sign my name and include the dealership's information, phone number and the hours that I worked. While my fellow salespeople were out trolling the lot trying to catch new customers, I was building relationships with the ones that I thought I could have. I sent cards to people who had not bought a car from me. I sent cards to people who had bought a car from me. I sent cards to parents, children, and siblings of anyone who came into the dealership. At first, the other employees of the dealership made endless fun of me because I was sending a birthday card almost every day. But I was diligent and hyperfocused. I saw the potential for success, and the success that I created all on my own—the success that no one else believed was possible. I had it in my grasp.

Finally, it all paid off. A young thirtysomething man strolled into the dealership. He was a stranger to us. He stepped in the door and looked skeptically from side to side. One of my fellow salesmen rose to greet him and shake his hand. The man said, "Hi. I'm, uh, looking for Leigh?"

CHAPTER TWENTY-THREE:

CADILLAC MAN

David Giwerc, founder of the ADD Coach Academy, insists that what you pay attention to grows.

> When you have a dominant negative thought, it creates the neuro-hormone adrenaline, which ignites the fight or flight response. If you continue to pay attention to the same negative thoughts without shifting away from the dominant pattern, it will over-activate your brain and exacerbate any anxiety, stress and worry that already exist. ("About..." p. 38 Volume 7:Number 3)

When you've grown up with ADHD and had a plethora of negative experiences, it can be challenging to filter out these negative thoughts. However, it is important to remember that you are in charge of creating your own positive space. The good news is, you don't have to do this alone.

If you're an adult with ADHD, find yourself a cheerleader. You may not even realize that it is your own negative thoughts that impede you from making progress, and that can leave you feeling hopeless. Having a cheerleader, someone to help you unearth the good in yourself, is essential. In my opinion, the best type of cheerleader is an ADHD Coach.

ADHD coaching is a relatively new field, although the premise behind the coaching aspect has been around for years. An ADHD Coach has studied ADHD specifically in his or her training. Many started as life coaches and then went on to specialize. Others, like my wife, wanted to know more about ADHD and how to help people and parents of children with it navigate through their lives in a positive, forward motion. Regardless of their reasoning, if becoming an ADHD specific coach, has gone through the proper channels for training, they will be well-qualified to be your best cheerleader.

With that being said, if you are a parent of a younger child with ADHD, your child is most heavily influenced by you. Therefore, the burden of building up your child's self-worth falls on you. Do not let them fall into the pattern of being consumed by negative thoughts. Remember that what you focus on will grow, so focus on their strengths and their passions and on what they do well. Consistently praise and highlight the positive accomplishments that he or she achieves, no matter how small or inconsequential they may seem.

Renee often uses this praise tactic on our youngest daughter. When she does something helpful or good that may seem insignificant to others, my wife is quick to point it out. For example, if she doesn't like the dress Renee has pulled out for her to wear, this can have resulted in an all-out war at our house. If my daughter dresses herself in something (no doubt unmatched and appalling by most standards) and hangs up the other dress in the closet instead of throwing a tantrum, she gets praised. Renee insists that it doesn't matter that she didn't wear what was put out for her or that she hung it up "incorrectly"; instead, she chooses to focus on the positives.

"Oh!" she says, "I love how you hung your dress up and put it back in the closet! That is excellent. Thank you for being so helpful today!" To an adult, it might sound ridiculous, insincere, or even condescending, but to our four-year-old, that is the best compliment she can imagine and she beams with pride.

Undoubtedly, it is difficult to be a parent that is that positive all of the time. However, if a child has just a few more "good cheers" to spur him or her on, that just may be enough to drive out the negatives.

I entered the car business feeling inadequate, low, and unfulfilled. I was sure that I was destined to be a failure. I failed at being a good son and a good brother. I failed at being well-liked and popular. I failed to graduate high school on time. It only made sense that I would also fail to graduate college. Ultimately, I had to drop out of college in my third year because my car was repossessed and I could no longer get to work to earn money to pay for tuition. I was 21 years old, and I was a giant failure.

Or was I?

Once I became a car salesman, I quickly learned a valuable lesson. I could actually control the outcome of my life. My past did not dictate who I could be in my future. Selling cars was the first time that I saw that I could get out of work and life whatever I put into them. Armed with this new revelation, I began to believe that I might not have to be the Spaz who fails. While working in the dealership with this new found hope, I began to earn money. Real money.

Obviously the paycheck was the overall motivating factor, but there was another benefit as well. I discovered that I enjoyed seeing people's lives improve because of something I had done for them. I got positive affirmation about my own life when I made someone else's life happier. Entrepreneur, author, and training expert, Grant Cardone, says, "Service is senior to selling", and while I did not know of Grant Cardone at the time, I was adopting this principle on a daily basis. If people feel well-served, they are more likely to buy.

I started developing my own strategies for selling cars. Rather than having a potential customer look at the car in the crowded, overwhelming lot, I would take them to the park on a test drive. While at the park, we would get out of the car and do a walk around. I showed them all the little features that people wouldn't normally notice.

Everything I pointed out demonstrated the superiority of the car above all others. At the end of our drive, even if the customer did not buy, they were satisfied. They were assured that they had received the best service possible. Initially, I was met with a lot of ridicule from my fellow employees. My methods weren't conventional—but then again, neither was I.

I excelled at selling cars through sheer determination. I went into work early. I stayed late. If I had a customer that wanted to come in on my day off, I went into work that day. It made me feel great that I had made someone else's life better by providing them with good service, and, hopefully, a good product.

Eventually, my fellow car salesmen began employing some of my tactics. However, they didn't work as well for them because they weren't genuine and authentic. My co-workers simply didn't have the motivation that I did. They didn't know what it was like to be a failure, at least not in the same way that I did. No one had told them that they should be dead or in jail. No one told them that they couldn't pass a course, go to college, make a sale. They had lives and identities outside of the car business that were meaningful. I'd built my life around service and selling.

In many ways you could say that I became hyperfocus on being a good car salesman. I took my all-or-nothing ADHD attributes and applied them wholeheartedly to my sales strategies. I could finally say that my ADHD was a positive driving force—a contributing factor in making me successful. I sold a lot of cars. I made a lot of friends. I had job offers coming out of my ears. I got a taste of success and I determined that failure, which had consumed my past, would not be my future.

CHAPTER TWENTY-FOUR:

DON'T PICK THE BOOGER

My wife teaches her clients that, in order to get someone with ADHD to do something, that something has to be their idea. She instructs that you can't tell someone with ADHD that they "have to" or "should" do something because those phrases are often met with resistance. Instead, if the idea stems from the mind of the ADHDer him or herself, they are far more likely to go along with it and see it through to the end.

Obviously this works much better in certain situations than in others. For instance, a fourth grader may not *choose* to do his or her homework, but they might want to choose when to have their allotted homework time or what type of project to do to fulfill an assignment. As much as parents want to control and even force the homework completion, it will always go much easier if the child can have some ownership over any/all aspects of it. This works well with projects too. Allowing children to choose their own topics gives them ownership. If they need to research a country and they choose some obscure one that you know nothing about just because they "have a pretty flag," don't try to convince them to choose a country that *you* know about. If something feels like it is their idea, they will want to see it through to the end.

I used to think that this was because certain kids are strong-willed, but it really has to do with interest. The thought behind this is, with interest, can come the ability to almost filter out the negative aspects of ADHD. If someone is fully engaged and interested in something, his or her brain would fire up that front cerebral cortex and be able to curb impulsivity and stimulate focus on the intended objective. When the interest level is high, therefore, someone with ADHD may look and behave like someone who does not have ADHD. Their intentions would be clear, their mind would be focused, they would have a plan for how to conquer the task. They would be able to filter out distractions and impulsive tendencies.

How can people with ADHD bottle up that interest and use it for everything they need to get done? I, too, am still working on the answer to that question.

In 1995 I was comfortably working as a salesman at a car dealership. At the age of 23, I was youngest salesman there. I was also one of the most successful. I thought it was time that I was recognized for my hard work, and I set about making that happen.

Most of my co-workers drove cars from the lot that we called "demos". They were new cars, and they came equipped with "Dealer" license plates. Unfortunately, I did not have a clean driving record and because of that, and my young age, the owner of the dealership did not give me a demo. To me, those demo cars were status symbols and I wanted one. Badly.

At the time I was driving a 4-door 1979 Toyota Corolla Tercel. The car was painted a metallic green with a yellow racing stripe over the top. The bumper-car green shade was probably from a spray can because it certainly did not look or last like automobile paint. The wheels were small. The top of the gear shifter was cleverly replaced with a black 8-ball. The interior color was a dingy brown but the front seats sported furry, tan seat covers. In order to drive it, I had to have the windows down because half of the muffler had rusted and fallen off from the catalytic converter. It was horribly loud, horribly ugly, and unfortunately the only car I could afford. My friends affectionately referred to it as "The Booger".

Although I drove "The Booger" to and from work, both the general manager and the owner of my dealership refused to let me park it on the lot. The car embarrassed them so much that I was asked to park around the corner so that potential customers did not see the car I was driving. I knew that all of my problems would be solved if I could only get my hands on a demo car, but in order to get one I had to be creative.

I began to notice that many customers inquired about what kind of car their salesperson owned. For most of my counterparts, this was a helpful selling point because they could gesture to their demo car or share its make and model, being careful to mention that it came from the dealership. This gave me a great idea. Gradually, I started parking "The Booger" closer and closer to the dealership. A customer of mine, who might be considering buying a brand new luxury automobile with all of its bells and whistles, would ask, "What kind of car do you drive?"

"Oh I drive that. Right there. That's my car," I'd say, as I gestured out the window towards "The Booger". I would do this when I knew the owner of the dealership was within earshot. Naturally, he *hated* it. Eventually, after a few months of using this tactic, the sales manager agreed to help me convince the owner that I needed a demo. Before he could do that however, I had to lower the points on my driving record. I had to take a Defensive Driving course.

I think that Defensive Driving course is the first class that I passed with flying colors. I hardly celebrated, however, because my mind was hyper focused on getting the demo. When the points on my driving record were erased and the certificate of the driving course was obtained, my sales manager had a meeting with the owner and the GM of auto dealership. After that meeting, I was awarded a used, black 1994 Mercury Tracer with manual roll-up windows.

It might as well have been a Mercedes Benz, a Porche, an Audi. That car took my self-esteem from zero to a thousand. When I sat in it and drove out of the dealership, I felt like I had made it in the world. The Mercury Tracer was the "win" I needed to propel me through the next years of my career. From that moment on, I knew that

I wanted to be even better. I was confident that I could shed the disappointments of my past and begin a life on the path of success. I was driven and focused in ways that I never knew were possible. I had shown myself what determination could accomplish and there was no stopping me from that point on. Finally, I was turning my disability into an ability.

CHAPTER TWENTY-FIVE:

LATHER. RINSE. REPEAT.

Boredom is dangerous. "Compared with the rest of us, they [people with ADHD] have sluggish and underfed brain reward circuits, so much of everyday life feels routine and under-stimulating. To compensate, they are drawn to new and exciting experiences and get famously impatient and restless with the regimented structure that characterizes our modern world" (Friedman). The ADHD brain *needs* stimulation, or else it is unable to filter out other aspects of the condition. Whereas a typical brain can understand and tolerate occasional lulls of inactivity, the ADHD brain feels enormous frustration and will seek to find a way to be stimulated.

Imagine a distractible girl in her second grade class. They are doing second grade math. She is highly intelligent, but not quite ready for a gifted and talented program or for alternative math outside of the regular classroom. She already knows how to do the day's lesson on subtracting three-digit numbers. Her brain is bored, so it has to create its own fun. In her head, she begins to weave a beautifully crafted story of a princess who is a warrior underneath and who fights battles in disguise. She might even sketch her princess, or just stare into the air as the story unfolds inside her brain. Just as the princess warrior is about to strike the final blow to the evil slug monster, a bell rings to signify that it is time for lunch. By then, she has missed the entire lesson, which might be OK since she already knew how to do it, but she has also missed instructions and directions. Perhaps she missed hearing about where they are going next in their studies, or if there is homework due the next day. What if she missed a field trip announcement and doesn't get her permission slip in on time? This scenario is typical of someone with inattentive-type ADHD.

Now picture a thirteen-year-old boy with hyperactive-type ADHD. He is swimming in a lake with friends. They are enjoying a day at their usual spot, swinging into the water on the rope swing, and joking around with one another. The other boys are lounging, eating, playing on their phones, and are content to go on the same rope swing over and over again. They try different releases, challenging one another to get the most air or to do the "sickest" trick. But the boy with ADHD has done the tricks before. He has mastered the rope, which seems embarrassingly low to him now, and he doesn't have any interest in the trite conversations around him. His eyes wander along the shore of the lake. He spots a tall tree a little ways off. Without telling anyone, he takes off his towel, and walks off towards the tree. He might get lost along his way. He might trip or hurts himself. Worse, he could make it to the tree, climb it, and then jump recklessly into the water, only to find that it is shallow and rocky underneath the surface, and his injuries are life-threatening.

This thrill-seeking behavior is common in people with ADHD. As young children, they are the climbers, the hitters, the biters. They constantly shave a couple of minutes off their parents' lives every day because they shock or scare them on a regular basis.

The common thread in these two seemingly different scenarios is listlessness. As people with ADHD grow older, we can generally figure out strategies to use to force ourselves to tolerate boredom. The current fidget gadget craze is the result of an attempt to find a solution to physical restlessness. A gifted and talented program or a vocational program that is challenging and/or new to someone can help to focus concentration and aid in coping with mental restlessness. However, nothing is guaranteed to work. Once again, we are faced with trial and error before we can find solutions that work for us. The good news is, trial and error can be pretty exciting!

I am like a cup of water with a tiny hole at the bottom. You can fill me up and fill me up and I will appear satiated, but slowly I will leak out of the bottom and need more water. I am never full and I require a constant steady stream of replenishment. This is an exhausting way to exist but it is the only way I know. Sometimes it leaves me feeling unsatisfied and depressed and other times it gives me the incentive I need to improve my life.

In the year 2000, I was having great success as a manager at an esteemed auto dealership. I was making six figures—the car business was booming and I was there to collect. I was good at my job. I had car sales down to a science, and I was far more successful than any of my elementary or high school teachers thought I would be. I most certainly was not dead or in jail and was well past the age of 18 so I felt I had conquered many demons from my past. I only wished that Dr. Smith could see me, so that he might rethink the suggestions he made for my 'treatment." In a nutshell, I had every reason to be happy.

But I was bored. I was tired of showing up to the same place every day. While I got to experience the different personalities of people who walked in the door, the processes that occurred once that happened was monotonously repetitive. Billing out a deal, penciling in a deal, ordering a car—it was all the same, over and over again. My daily life was full of repetition. Consequently, after a couple of years, I found it all to be extremely boring.

My job was also very restrictive, in my opinion. I wanted some freedom. I needed something more interesting. I yearned for new challenges. I desired change. I found myself growing less and less satisfied with my sales job. I knew if I did not take action that little cloud of depression that I just barely kept at bay would creep in over my head once again. It did not matter that I was making more money than anyone I knew ever dreamed possible. I simply was not happy.

The problem was, I didn't have a lot of marketable skills. I'd joined the car sales industry because it accepted me when no one else would. I lacked a college degree and this automatically disqualified me from just about any job I could fathom. The only solution was, do the unfathomable. I was about to dive into the world of finance.

I knew a former employee, Tom, who'd left the car dealership to work for a bank. He still did financial business with car dealers. I was accustomed to the representatives from various banks visiting our dealerships and trying to get us to use them for finances the cars we sold. It was not long after he left auto sales that Tom rolled back into my dealership to try to acquire some loan applications. I knew that his wife was pregnant when he'd left so I greeted him with a smile.

"How's the baby?"

"Oh he's great! Just great. I actually just had him with me on a couple of calls to give my wife a break," he replied enthusiastically.

"What?" I wasn't sure I'd understood what he meant.

"Yeah. I get a lot of freedom in this job. I make my own hours and sometimes I can bring him with me when I visit stores. I cover a large geographical area so sometimes I have to drive a lot, but I'm really loving it."

Freedom. He'd said "freedom". He'd described something that was completely lacking in my current situation. I was stuck at the dealership. It was not even guaranteed that I would have a day off. I had set hours. I could not venture out of the store to do business. I most certainly could not bring a baby with me to work—not that I had one at the time—but still! Freedom. Tom's gleeful smile as we continued to make small talk confirmed that I needed what he had.

To leave car sales at that time was ludicrous because everyone was making so much money. The economy was thriving and people were buying cars left and right. Tom's new position as a Dealer Relations Manager did not pay nearly what I was currently making at the dealership. However, I realized that I couldn't put a price on happiness. Besides, the economy could collapse at any moment (trust me, I thought about this "what if" every day), and I would be struggling to pay my bills with no degree to fall back on. I had to find a way to be in charge of my own future. I wanted to have that freedom to design my own life. Most importantly, I needed something that would hold my attention.

A couple of days later, the representative from a competing auto finance company came into my store. Mark was out scouting dealerships to sign to do business with this bank. This company was new to the market. It specialized in prime lending (customers with good credit), and in 2000, prime banks were in excess. It was nearly impossible to do well because there was so much competition. As a bank that was new to our area, they were not performing exceptionally well and neither was Mark. I thought of Tom and his newfound freedom. Then I looked at Mark, struggling in the same role, but with a different bank and totally lacking the ability to form the relationships he needed with the dealers in order to do his job. I thought, "I could do this. I could do this well." I already had relationships with dealers throughout my state. When I took in a vehicle as a trade, I would shop other dealers to find out who was going to give me the most money for it. Therefore, I was in touch with many local dealerships on a regular basis and I already had a network of dealers without ever having to leave my dealership. I was one step ahead of Mark, and I was brimming with curiosity about the possibility of switching industries to the banking side.

Mark told me that he was looking for someone to work for the automotive lending side and represent several nearby states. He mentioned that the bank had tellers and physical offices in some areas but not in others. He also admitted that they had no dealers willing to sign up with them because of this and the saturated prime lending market.

I immediately told him that I was interested in the job. "Look," I began, "I already have relationships with these dealers so I can get my foot in the door. After that, I just have to sell them on signing with our bank. If I can do anything, I can sell." His clammy-skinned face looked vaguely intrigued. He asked me a few non-specific questions and then he asked the one I dreaded most,

"Where did you go to school?"

I named my high school and laughed. I tried to distract him with humor to keep him from asking the question I most wished to avoid. No such luck.

"No. Where did you get your degree?"

"Well, I finished three years of college, but…"

"Eh. This job probably isn't for you," he grunted. "There are a lot of numbers and whatnot involved. Plus, you'd have to travel a lot, you wouldn't make much money with no stores signed up, and a college degree is kind of a requirement." His tone told me that he had already dismissed me. "But here's my business card and all the info you need about signing your store up with our bank so just call me if you have any questions about that." With that, he got up and shuffled out the door.

I was not to be deterred, however. I tucked his business card off to the side of my desk and mulled over my predicament for about a week. Finally, I developed a plan. I figured I could get his attention the same way I'd gotten everyone else's attention my entire life. I would annoy him. For the next several days, whenever I would get a credit application from another lender, not only would I follow through and fax it off to the necessary people, but I would also fax it to Mark's fax phone number on his business card. I wasn't trying to use his bank or do business with him. I was trying to irritate him—and it worked. Before long, the phone on my desk rang.

"Ah Leigh, Mark here. I think you made a mistake. I've been getting these credit applications for competing lenders coming across my fax. I think you might be sending them to the wrong fax number."

"Mark! Hey! Auto finance, right?"

"Yeah. That's right," he mumbled.

"Oh man. I don't know how you ended up with those

applications. Sorry about that. I must've sent them to the wrong fax number." I paused but before he could speak I asked, "Did you hire anyone yet?" I could hear the faintest chuckle emerge from him.

"Are you kidding me right now?" he asked.

"No. I'm serious," I insisted.

"You deliberately sent me these applications, didn't you?"

"Yes I did, sir," I said matter-of-factly. "When can you set up an interview for me?" I heard the sigh of a man who was beaten.

"Oh for Christ's sakes. You MFer!" he said almost affectionately. (Little did I know that "MFer" would become his nickname for me and when he would call me in the future he would always begin with "What up MFer?") "Let me see what I can do." And with that, we said our goodbyes and I went about my day. I thought that at the very least he would remember me for future opportunities, in case something came up that wouldn't require that all-important college degree. But lo and behold, the following Monday I received a call asking me to fly out for an interview with the company's National Sales Manager.

I brought my natural bravado with me to that interview, and I told the National Sales Manager that I would sign 84 accounts in the first 120 days. I would basically take their business from zero accounts to 84 in my first four months. Plus, I vowed to have at least half of them producing deals in that time. He laughed at me. He told me that there was no way I could do that. I replied with, "If I don't do it in 120 days, you can fire me. When can I start?" He laughed again. I didn't know if I would get the job, but I was confident in my determination and ability to do it. I started calling the dealers that I already had a relationship with. Within a couple of days, I had the names of over forty finance managers at the stores with which I was already familiar.

The next week, the NSM called to offer me the job. Although he didn't mention my stipulation of 84 accounts, I kept it locked inside my head. After thirty days on the job, I had signed half. After 120 days, I had over 90 accounts signed with this bank. I wasn't going anywhere.

I had talked my way into a job that required a college degree, which I didn't have. It was a job that would pay me significantly less money than I was making at the dealership, but it was a job that, to me, promised an interesting and exciting future. And that was all my ADHD brain wanted.

CHAPTER TWENTY-SIX:

HOW TO GET
WELL(BUTRIN)

An article on the popular site, WebMD, lists the 10 most common symptoms of Adult ADHD as: poor listening skills, extreme distractibility, marital difficulties, trouble getting organized, reckless driving/accidents, restlessness/trouble relaxing, trouble starting a task, angry outbursts, and issues prioritizing ("10 Problems…"). I look at this list and I feel like it is misleading.

Poor listening skills? We are listening…just not to you: or to anything that isn't interesting to us. ADHD is selective hearing at its finest. Extreme distractibility? As adult ADHDers, we are constantly multitasking, so it's nearly impossible to keep fully focused on any one thing. Marital difficulties? Only if you're married to someone who does not understand your ADHD. Trouble getting organized? Organization in the traditional sense of the word is not our strong point, but I would argue that most of us ADHDers have our own version of organization. It may not make sense to the rest of the world, but it works for us. Reckless driving/accidents? This actually may be true, but it's only because we are running late to get everywhere. Trouble starting a task? This depends on the task. I don't have any problems starting certain tasks. I am a motivated worker and I thrive on getting things done. Do I occasionally experience procrastination or perfection paralysis? Sure—but doesn't everyone? Angry outbursts? Though these can happen, I would not say that they are something that occur commonly that that should make the top ten list. Issues prioritizing? What in the world does this even mean? Issues prioritizing what? While I may not love paying bills, I am always sure to do it before being charged any late fees.

Obviously everyone's ADHD will manifest in different ways. I am not suggesting that the aforementioned list is wrong, but I do feel like it doesn't represent my struggles. I tried to think of my own list and came up with these three personal challenges: thinking too fast, trouble recognizing boundaries, and comprehension difficulties.

Thinking too fast has its pros and cons. On the positive side, a fast-paced brain helps me accomplish a great deal in a short amount of time. This also helps me multitask effectively. I can watch television, type on the computer, and listen to an audiobook at the same time. While I'm not giving any of those things my undivided attention, I am still able to pay attention to everything. The negative aspect of thinking too fast is that sometimes things get missed or go unnoticed. If it is not a pressing issue or something that is occurring in the distant future, I will think right on by it. Additionally, thinking too fast can be off-putting to others, but I grew up in an area where people tend to be in a rush to go or get anywhere. Even the pace of my speech is rapid because it matches how fast the thoughts are churning in my head. When my family and I relocated to the south, I experienced my own person Civil War with my rapid, hyper, northern Yankee-style verses the slow, easy-going, languid southern style. It took me a little while to adapt to the unhurried way of handling things. If I am given control over anything, however, I expect those around me to move at my pace, and that is not always comfortable for them.

Boundaries are a challenge for me because if I think of something right away, I'll handle it right away. If this means that I need to make a work phone call at 8:45pm on a Friday, that is what I will do. This obviously rubs some people the wrong way. I understand that, and yet I never stop and take that into consideration. I don't know if it is due to impulsivity or a fear that I will become distracted and forget whatever it is I had in mind, but I do know that I generally violate traditionally accepted boundaries more often than not. I might also take a call in the middle of a dinner or party. This is because, while I don't set up boundaries for myself, I also do not set them up for other people. Just as I would expect someone else to take my 8:45pm phone call on a Friday night, I will stop everything to handle a business matter, because I have not set up a boundary between business and pleasure. Like thinking too fast, this can have its advantages. I clearly get things accomplished because of my lack of boundaries. I come across as a hard and dedicated worker (which I am), and I make a great salesperson. However, my lack of boundaries can result in people thinking I'm pushy, careless, and self-centered.

I have learned to recognize thinking too fast and difficulty with boundaries as flaws of mine, even though they can work to my advantage. However, it is hard to see the upside of comprehension difficulties. In "Finite Math", I discovered that I learned differently while I was in college. While I knew that I learned differently from a young age, it wasn't until adulthood that I truly realized what that meant. I am a "do-er". The way I retain something is to physically do it, and I can also learn by listening while doing. In most classroom settings, students are expected to read something and retain it. However, my distractibility makes this model impossible for me to achieve successfully.

In my early thirties, I happened across an audio version of "How to Win Friends and Influence People," by Dale Carnegie. I also happened to have the physical, hardcover book as well. Every day on my way to and from work, at the gym, before bed, and even on the toilet, I consumed the audio content. Then I found myself reading the actual book! Not only did I read a book cover to cover for the first time in my life, I also understood it and had clarity on the content. I realized then that I could actually get enjoyment from reading. If I was able to listen to the audio version first, there was nothing stopping me from finishing the material and retaining it. Now, I read 30-40 books a year using this method.

The positive aspect of your individual learning

challenges will only come when you understand how you personally learn best. Once you capture this nugget of information, you will be unstoppable. Until then you may struggle, but I promise the struggle will make you stronger in the end. Keep trying. Keep learning. Keep staying true to yourself and your needs. You will not regret it.

By the age of 26, I thought of myself as an ethical version of Jay Gatsby. I was a young man without a college degree, living alone on a six-figure salary. Since I was not accustomed to that type of wealth, I fell into the typical traps of being "new money." I spent, I partied, I worked hard—but I didn't have my Daisy yet. I thought I'd found her when I met my first wife through mutual friends at a restaurant. She was a manager at a high-end car dealership and I was the manager of another high-end dealership. We were two peas in a pod—two Type-A hard working young adults who reveled in the finer things our money and positions brought us.

We were married less than two years after we met. Rather than spending our money on a wedding, we got married by a justice of the peace in a park. This was the same park where, just seven years prior, I had gone to contemplate ending my life. Then we took a month-long honeymoon to travel. We were young, in love, and successful. What could go wrong?

Unfortunately, a year into our marriage, we discovered that we were not as compatible as we'd originally thought. Working in the same industry was initially a fun commonality, but it began to feel like a competition. I didn't understand this side of her just as I am sure she did not understand some of my personality quirks. When we weren't working, she and I spent time going out and clubbing. I had taken up disc jockeying when I wasn't working at the dealership and I was good at it. I had secured a residential DJ spot at one of the hottest nightclubs in our area and I was opening for big names and/or playing the whole night away myself. As with every other job, I threw myself into the DJ scene, and I focused a great deal of my attention on selling myself to promoters, getting other gigs, and finding the next best piece of equipment or music to play. While I was hyperfocused on DJ-ing, I lost sight of our marriage and what my wife was doing while I was busy spinning.

By the late 1990's my wife and I continued to grow apart. We were both making six-figure salaries and enjoying the luxuries of being young and childless, but we argued incessantly. The fights that would ensue after the partying and the late nights were exhausting. In some ways, I was still that scared boy who had been tossed in the dumpster in fourth grade, and I felt as though I let her walk all over me as I had done with the kids back then. Once I knew that I wanted out of the marriage, I was too scared to go. I had no place to live and no money that was separate from our joint account which she monitored. I refused to live (un)happily ever after. I knew how it ended for Jay Gatsby and I needed to get out

before that happened. To do that, I needed to get myself back on track.

The only things that brought me any semblance of joy were DJ-ing and my job at the car dealership, and I was quickly losing interest in the latter. A good friend of mine knew a little bit about what I dealing with, and he talked me into seeing a psychiatrist. I did not want to admit to others that I needed a psychiatrist or that I could be depressed because it was very difficult for me to accept that something was "wrong" with me. After years of being told that I wouldn't amount to anything, I had amounted to something. I had a successful career and a lovely wife. I feared that once people discovered that my "perfect life" had flaws, I'd be labeled as a failure once again.

After two meetings with the psychiatrist, I felt certain that he knew my entire life story. He read the notes from my overnight visits to the hospital when I was younger, my history of ADHD and Ritalin, and the birth and passing of my youngest brother who was believed to be autistic, and he diagnosed me with Asperger Syndrome. It was only after I got home and researched the term that I saw that it was a form of autism. I was shocked and angry at being labeled once again. Wasn't the ADHD enough? The psychiatrist prescribed me Wellbutrin "a prescription medicine used to treat adults with a certain type of depression called major depressive disorder, and for the prevention of autumn-winter seasonal depression (seasonal affective disorder)" ("Wellbutrin"). Although it has occasionally been prescribed for ADHD, it is not something that is commonly thought to help with the challenges of someone with that disorder. Given my past experience with medications, I was reluctant to take anything at all, but I did know a couple of people who were on Wellbutrin. They told me that it had worked for them, and recommended that I try it. At that point, I was willing to try anything to feel better, so I started on the medication.

I was in a new job by then, having transitioned from the car business to the indirect lending side with an auto finance company. I covered a large territory so there was a lot of driving and travel involved in this position. Part of this job was developing relationships with car dealerships. In order to do so, it meant stopping in and visiting various dealers throughout the day. The more loan originations I could get the more commission I could make and that was obviously a huge incentive to go into as many dealerships as possible. I had not been at this job for long, but I was already pretty good at it. My hyper personality enabled me to go tirelessly from one store to the next, and my constant need to be in motion (physically and mentally) fueled my desire to get in and out as quickly and efficiently as possible.

After about a week on the Wellbutrin I found myself driving past a Hyundai dealership that I'd been meaning to stop and visit. I looked out of my driver's side window and watched it pass by. "I'll just call them next week," I thought to myself. The thought shocked me. It did not feel like the Leigh Macneil I had become. Prior to that week, I'd had a burning desire to finish everything

I started. This desire developed over the course of my adolescence when I realized that if I didn't complete something immediately, I would never go back and complete it later. I never stopped until I'd done what I'd set out to do.

Therefore, this new procrastination was completely out of character for me. The sense of urgency that I was accustomed to had vanished. I thought back over the past couple of days and realized that I had been living in a world of "if it happens, it happens" rather than the "I have to get it done" mentality that I usually had. This Hyundai dealership was not the first one I had skipped, and I hadn't completed my call notes from three days ago. The routine work day that I had set up for myself, the one that guaranteed my success, was completely altered.

This was not ok with me. Failure was not an option.

It took less than two months of taking the Wellbutrin for my loan numbers to begin dropping. My paycheck took a dramatic hit. Although physically I felt fine, I realized that I was just not built to live a laid-back life. The sense of urgency I was born with had dissipated due to the medication. I visited the psychiatrist again. He agreed that I could go off of Wellbutrin. When he suggested other medicinal options, I declined them all. I might not have been living the happiest of lives at that moment in time, but I was going to get through it like I always did—full steam ahead. There would be no more "I'll just do it next week". For the rest of my life there would only be "I'll do it now". The first step was to turn my back on the green light at the end of Daisy's dock. It was time to stop re-living my past failures. I was ready to say goodbye to my marriage and hello to my future.

CHAPTER TWENTY-SEVEN:

IT'S ALL GOOD, BABY

"ADHD runs in families. Anywhere from one-third to one-half of parents with ADHD will have a child with the disorder. There are genetic characteristics that seem to be passed down. If a parent has ADHD, a child has more than a 50% chance of having it. If an older sibling has it, a child has more than a 30% chance." ("Attention Deficit...")

When this information is given to a parent of a child with ADHD, the most natural reaction is for them to blame themselves. During the time she's been coaching, my wife has often heard stories of parents who have had their child diagnosed, only find out that they also suffer from the disorder. While it can be challenging to have one ADHD person in the family, it can be nearly disastrous to have two unless parents can learn to manage their own ADHD effectively.

I don't know where the ADHD in my family comes from. Neither of my parents seem to have had it, and they certainly didn't recognize it immediately when it surfaced in me as a young boy. But I do know that it must exist in my family tree somewhere. I know I have some family history with alcoholism. Addiction and ADHD can be closely linked. It's certainly possible that some of them had my disorder.

No matter where it comes from, it is important to realize that people with ADHD can live very successful lives. The child who was distracted in the classroom may become an adult who takes a job that allows them to travel and change their scenery day after day. The child who felt a constant bombardment of thoughts, causing them mental restlessness and anxiety, could grow up to become an incredible investigator, reporter, or nurse. That fast-paced mind is uniquely suited for problem-solving from many different viewpoints. Learning how to use your ADHD to your advantage can be amazingly effective and rewarding. Before you can do this, however, you have to admit that you need some help understanding and managing your ADHD.

My wife is convinced that she could tell that our first daughter, Isabelle, had ADHD before she was born. She jokes that Isabelle paid no attention to due dates even then. She remained breech long enough for my poor wife to undergo hours of lying upside down on an ironing board (a strategy that, believe it or not, the doctor advised us to try) in order to turn her around. When her due date came and went, my wife grew irritable and nervous. A week later, we went to the hospital to prep for an induction the next morning, but Isabelle was already on her way on her own schedule.

When she was born, she was the most alert baby anyone had ever seen. Countless people visited our hospital room expecting to cuddle a sleeping newborn, but were greeted by a wide-eyed, observant little bundle. She hardly cried. She hardly slept. We adored every waking hour with her.

Initially, upon discovering that my wife was pregnant, I silently prayed for us to have a girl. Although I would not have a boy to carry on the family name or to follow my lead in the male-dominated world of mixed martial arts, I needed our new addition to be a girl. I had developed a deep-seeded fear that, if we had a son, he would be just like me. I *knew* that a male Macneil would struggle with ADHD, and I couldn't bear the thought of passing it on to my own child. I did not want to be responsible for him growing up with the same stigmas that I did. I did not want him to think that he had no hope of a successful future, and I certainly did not want to be the one to tell him at a young age that the world could be a cruel place to someone like him.

At the twenty-week ultrasound, when the technician said she was 85% sure that our baby was a girl (of course, little Isabelle had not been cooperating enough to show her private parts to the screen), I felt a sense of relief wash over me. I had not shared my fears with my wife, so she was immediately concerned that I would be disappointed by the news. I assured her, with tears in my eyes, that I was beyond thrilled about the 85% possibility of Baby Girl Macneil.

I'm not sure why I assumed that only a boy could have ADHD, although at the time statistics did show that boys are about three times more likely to be diagnosed with ADHD than girls. I simply assumed that the odds were in our favor. It is now believed that anywhere from one third to one half of adults with ADHD will pass the trait on to their children. "If a parent has ADHD, a child has more than a 50% chance of having it" ("Attention Deficit"). If I had known this, I probably would not have relaxed so much.

As Isabelle grew, I dismissed her impulsive, hyper behavior and inattentiveness as signs of a spoiled child. I knew we were in a position to provide much more to her than I ever had and she certainly did not want for anything. If she got into trouble, I thought she needed more discipline or fewer possessions as a consequence. My wife knew better. She knew that Isabelle's impulsive reactions, spacey hyper-focus, anxiety, constant need to be in motion, irrational mood swings, and difficulty sleeping stemmed from something deeper than a lack of discipline. She knew that Isabelle was my mini-me. She knew even when I refused to see it.

Now that our "little bundle" is in elementary school, she is thriving with the help and support provided to her by her Individualized Education Plan (IEP) created by her school's special education department. These days they have a category for people like us: Other Health Impaired. ADHD is no longer a sentence of "death or jail by the time you're eighteen." Doctors have finally learned that there is a neurological reason why some people act, think, and learn differently, and the disorder is embraced in its legitimacy. Isabelle will have the support she needs to be successful and, when she is, she will be so *because* of her ADHD, not in spite of it.

CHAPTER TWENTY-EIGHT:

I'LL BE AT THE COOL ADULTS TABLE

The United States Equal Opportunity Employment Commission (EEOC) was founded to protect people from discrimination in the workplace. This commission combined with the Americans with Disabilities Act of 1990, makes it illegal to discriminate against qualified individuals with disabilities in job applications, hiring, firing, compensation, and other areas of the working environment. On its website the EEOC states:

> "It is illegal to harass an applicant or employee because he has a disability, had a disability in the past, or is believed to have a physical or mental impairment that is not transitory (lasting or expected to last six months or less) and minor (even if he does not have such an impairment)." (*Disability Discrimination*)

It is tremendously important that adults with ADHD know that there are laws out there to protect them, not only in an educational setting, but also in the workplace. We hear jokes about ADHD all too often. Because it is not a visible disability, people still laugh about and question the validity of ADHD all too frequently. While it may be protected by new special education and equal employment laws, people outside of those parameters don't always treat ADHDers kindly. Because we have been conditioned to be sensitive and empathetic to people with visible disabilities, they seem more protected by the laws. Even though research has proven that ADHD is a neurological condition and, therefore one that is incurable and not self-inflicted, many people do not even know that it is considered a disability.

I learned early on that, in order to survive in the world, I had to make light of things that were really and truly dark. I became a class clown and a goofy trouble-maker. I thought if I could make people laugh, then they would want me around despite my ADHD and all its challenges. While people made fun of me, I decided that I could cope if I could laugh it off. And, ultimately, I made the most fun of myself. I wonder how different my life would have been if I called one of my taunters out, educated them a bit on what characteristics of ADHD I had and why they made me behave a certain way, and let them know that, while I could take a joke, it didn't mean that I always *was* the joke.

Educating people about ADHD is essential. If you, your child, your spouse, or loved one has ADHD, I urge you to arm yourself with as much information as you can. This book is a great start! But, if you or someone you know is concerned about your treatment in the workplace and think it is because you are being discriminated against due to your ADHD, the U.S Equal Employment Opportunity Commission, EEOC, is a great resource so check it out and get to know your rights: https://www. eeoc.gov.

For some reason I assumed that, when I reached adulthood, I would never feel like a failure or a loser again. To some degree I could understand why my middle school and high school peers made fun of me, ostracized me, or just thought I was plain weird. I was different—that was for sure. But I figured that adults would be more understanding and accepting. I was wrong.

Once I proved myself in the workforce in one position, I really felt determined to try to move up the ladder. I had found an industry that I was successful in and had worked my way up to a position where I had nine employees working underneath me. I had a wife and two beautiful children who had relocated with me three years prior when I'd earned my first big promotion. I was one of the top performers in my company. I had a reputation for being the guy who got things done. People in my company respected me and my efforts. I often received phone calls from other managers in the company who would ask about my methods, because my numbers were so high. I was getting a lot of attention internally and it was obvious that I was in line for another step up the corporate ladder, so I put my name in for a promotion to a Vice President.

I flew to headquarters for my interview. All of the four candidates were there interviewing at the same time. We all knew each other so it was a bit awkward that we flew in together and even ate lunch together. I felt really confident about my performance and proud of how I had interviewed. After seven years with the company, I knew my stuff. I was invested in bettering the business. Prior to my interviews, the person who could become my boss had honestly led me to believe that I was going to get the position. I felt that it was my job to lose; I had the track record behind me that proved that I was the best person available.

A week went by, and no one heard anything. The other candidates and I were friendly enough that we constantly texted and checked in with one another, but none of us had anything to report. Finally, all four of us received a generic "Thanks but no thanks" email. It turns out that they'd gone with an outside candidate that none of us knew. I felt pretty disgruntled, but we all moved on and settled back into our respective positions.

Another week went by and suddenly I found myself on the phone with one of the higher ups. He called me and said, "Hey Leigh, you still may have a shot at this job! The outside candidate turned it down." I was elated. I felt certain that I would get the offer. However, the promotion was awarded to one of the other original interviewees. I was shocked, and I think everyone else was too. I replayed my interviews over and over again in my head, and I could not figure out where I had gone wrong. I would have ruminated forever had I not received a phone call from one of the senior employees in the company.

He had been one of the interviewers. I knew him pretty well at that point. I felt that we had a good relationship, even though he was more of an outgoing, party-animal-man's-man and I was more of a keep-to-myself-buckle-down-go-to-bed-by-nine kind of guy. But I did feel like we had a mutual respect for one another. We made some small talk and then he said,

"You did great in your interviews! All of the VPs thought you did awesome." I was a bit taken aback.

"Thanks," I stammered, unsure of where he was going.

"Yeah, we just really need to work on slowing you down. You know, sometimes you have to slow down to speed up."

"I'm not really following," I said.

"Well you are, you know, just sort of an intimidating guy. You're really intense. We need to tone that down a little. I can help coach you." I didn't know how to respond. Perhaps if I had paused a moment and really thought about it, I might have played the game, laughed it off, and accepted his offer to "coach" me through learning to slow down. Of course, I did not pause. I did not process and try to filter my response. I reacted.

"But I'm not that guy! This is who I am." Before he could interject, I plowed on, "That intensity is what has made me so successful. If I wasn't that intense, I would be just as mediocre as all the other candidates. My performance is good because I am intense. My performance is good because I'm driven and because I hyperfocus." There was a brief silence and then a chuckle.

"Oh I know. I know. That's why I love you! *I* think you're great." There was another chuckle on his end. This time I could read the discomfort in it. "Anyway, so here's what this week will look like …" and he continued on in his normal fashion completely dropping the subject and the suggestions he had made.

For me, though, the subject was not dead. I thought back to when I applied for the position in my current job and my boss at the time told me that he was afraid I might be "too face-paced" to be in a management role. Had he really meant the same thing that my current boss did? Were they really saying that I was "too ADHD"?

The way I looked at it, I had two choices. I could curb my exuberance and "slow down" as was suggested, or I could work ten times harder and become even better, so that there would be no way I could be ignored or passed over ever again. I chose the latter. I doubled my efforts and increased my team's visibility in the company. By the end of the year, I had earned an award for my region, which won my wife and I a trip to a beautiful resort. Just after that announcement came, there was an opening for a Vice President in a different region. It meant relocation. It meant my wife would have to leave her job. It meant my oldest daughter would switch schools and leave her friends. But it also meant that I could show everyone that being "too ADHD" was not my disability. It was the *ability* I had that I could hone into in order to be successful at my job.

I was flown back for another interview. I displayed the same vigor and enthusiasm that I had before. I answered the same questions in the same way. I was not shy about my "aggressive" style of getting things done. I was an intense as ever. I had the numbers to prove that my style worked.

That time I got the job.

CHAPTER TWENTY-NINE:

THIS IS YOUR BRAIN ON ADHD

"Do not allow negative thoughts to enter your mind for they are the weeds that strangle confidence."—Bruce Lee

Some people with ADHD experience what is known as "rumination". According to the Merriam Webster Dictionary, to "ruminate" is "to go over in the mind repeatedly and often casually or slowly" ("Ruminate"). While this may sound unlike a typical brain with hyperactivity, this type of rumination is different than pausing or controlling impulsivity. Rumination, in this case, is ceaselessly repeating *negative* thoughts in the brain. I refer to these as the "what ifs". An ADHD mind gets fixated on "what if" something bad/negative were to happen, and then it is unable to break away from those thoughts. The person gets stuck on negative scenarios and outcomes and cannot move forward with whatever action needs to take place at the moment.

Like all traits of ADHD, rumination can be managed.

Different tactics work for different people. Something that I like to use is called the "Five People Plan". It is not something that I invented; my wife learned of it from the ADD Coach Academy. I think it is quite clever and very effective. The idea is simple. Tell one person what you're ruminating on. This may look like you're venting, stressing, or simply anxious, but let it all out. Their response is actually irrelevant to this exercise. Next, tell a second person the same thing, and so on. Once you get to your fifth person, you're done ruminating about whatever it is that you were worrying about because you've just talked yourself silly about it. You simply get tired of yourself!

Again, everyone is different and will have different strategies to tackle the problems that arise with ADHD. You just want to make sure you have a hefty bag of strategies to choose from.

My brain never shuts off.

I know that's a bit of a cliché. A lot of people will tell you that they feel the same way. They will say that they think too much or that they're always worrying about something. They will try to joke that maybe they have ADHD too. People who say this never realize how much of an insult that is to someone who has my brain. The true ADHD brain is complicated beyond comprehension. If I have something I am scheduled to do, something on my calendar or a plan I have to execute, I am consumed by thoughts of that event. I fixate on scenarios. My brain will run through the "what-ifs" over and over and over again. Once I decide to hone in on one of the what-ifs, it turns into, "What will I do next? What will that be and what will that look like?" Then, of course, I have to speculate: "What if that 'what-if' doesn't work out? What will be the next piece? What's my next 'what-if'?"

If I had to articulate what this is like, I'd say that it feels like friction. It feels as though something is rubbing together so hard, as if someone is trying to start a fire, that it eventually creates a spark, heat, tension or a pulse in my brain. Something is grinding in my head and my body like a deep tissue massage in the same spot over and over again. I am incredibly anxious and I need to complete that task, whatever it may be, or else the machine that is my brain will explode. If I try to distract myself, I may be able to focus on something else on the surface, but the grinding feeling will not let up. This feeling constantly replays itself and I feel as if I am in motion, even if I am sitting perfectly still. There is no reprieve.

When my "what-ifs" come into my head, I become irrational. If I have a purpose and a task ahead, it does not leave my mind. It may seem as though I am flighty, forgetful, or self-absorbed about other things, but that is not the case. Those things are not part of that grinding feeling. They are not on replay in my head. I can address other situations and can even occasionally handle them successfully, but I am never fully present in those moments.

Unfortunately, my family bears the brunt of this. It is not that I am forgetful or unconcerned with them in fact, the opposite is true. Most of my tasks ultimately revolve around making their lives better, safer, or more comfortable. It's just that whatever all-consuming scenario is in my head won't allow me to ignore it, won't allow me peace, until it is accomplished. I am simultaneously stressing about my "what-ifs" while planning out how I will conquer them. I can go home and encircle my daughters in my arms and think about what I will do to protect them, but my mind will grind away about tomorrow's meeting. Even though they are the center of my "what if" world the constant "what ifs" can often take me out of the most precious moments of my life.

CHAPTER THIRTY

RENEE AND SPAZ SITTIN' IN A TREE

Statistics for failed marriages between an ADHD spouse and a non-ADHD spouse are astronomically high. There are numerous articles, blogs, and even entire books written listing the reasons why marriages fail and how to prevent them from doing so. It is not difficult to decipher the reasons why marriages with one ADHD spouse fail. The laundry lists of reasons you will find out there are simply the very same complaints about ADHD in general. People with ADHD are seemingly self-centered, disorganized and forgetful (of anniversaries, birthdays, or other important dates and events), impulsive and \quick to anger. He could marry, or even stray, on a whim. He could become addicted to drugs, porn, gambling, food, and/or spending. He could hyperfocus on something that does not involve his mate or his family causing them to feel left-out, unloved, and unimportant. Additionally, he could feel like his spouse's child rather than their equal, especially when it comes to chores, listening, and following through with what he said he was going to do.

Given the list of short comings, it is no wonder that so many ADHDer's marriages fail. The divorce rate in the United States is already high. A 2016 article in *Time Magazine* stated, "researchers have found that typical marriages still have about a 50% chance of lasting" ("Divorce Rate..."). With a typical marriage at only a 50% chance of lasting, you may be asking yourself "What chance does an ADHDer's marriage have?" The truth is, it has the same chance as any other marriage *if* you marry the right person. While I cannot tell you who you need to ensure that you have a successful marriage, I can assure you that Googling "how to make an ADHD marriage last" will not tell you either.

I am not a romantic, but if the story of why my marriage works will help others, then I will tell it. I hope it makes people with ADHD realize that someone will love them and their ADHD, even though they may not have always loved themselves. If there is someone out there for me, then I truly believe there has to be someone out there for everyone.

Our marriage is not perfect. There are many things about me that Renee would probably change if she could. But, since she can't, she has made a real effort to understand not just *how* my mind works, but also *why*. You see, the *why* creates understanding. If an ADHDer can find someone willing to understand his *why*, then he has found a treasure. When someone takes the time to learn about him and his quirks, be they associated with his ADHD or not, that partner will accept that there is a reason for the quirks and they will love the ADHDer in spite of them. Or maybe even because of them. In order to write this, Renee and I really had to think about our relationship. This is when I learned that she has taken great care to understand me, and my how and why. Understanding my ADHD has always been a priority for Renee. And for that, I am forever grateful.

Women are the devil. This is what I thought in early 2005. A failed marriage and limited experience in serious relationships were enough to convince me that I did not want to become entangled in any woman's twisted web. I was working hard and finding success in the auto industry. I had purchased my very own townhouse. I still DJed from time to time, but most of my out-of-work down time was spent training and fighting mixed martial arts. With my black belt in Judo and Small Circle Jujitsu, my wrestling background, and some Muai Tai kickboxing training under my belt, mixed martial arts had an obvious draw for me. At this time, MMA was thriving so I had no shortage of places to train, people to train with, or fight cards to accept.

During my first marriage, I stepped away from martial arts and ultimate fighting. My single life, however, afforded me plenty of time to get back into training and then back into the ring. It was not long after I resumed training that I was able to fight professionally. With professional fighting came many female fans and gorgeous ring girls, but my mind was not interested in them. I worked my day job tirelessly and I worked my night job of training, fighting, and eating clean religiously. There was little time for a woman, even a flashy one in a bikini posing for pictures with me and my trophy. And besides, they were the devil.

And then I met Renee.

She was beautiful, kind and funny. She was a high school teacher who had a Master's degree and she acted with community theaters in her spare time. She ordered nachos on our first date even though I wasn't ordering anything to eat. She lived by herself with her pit bull mix in an apartment and completely supported herself on her meager teacher's salary. She was completely unimpressed by materialistic or name brand things. She was athletic and confident and she was definitely not the devil.

This put me into a tailspin. I was in a good place in my life and I wasn't sure I wanted anything to change. But at the same time, I wanted everything to change. I knew almost instantly that I loved her although it would take me a week and a half to tell her. Fortunately, she loved me too. After one month of dating she was practically living in my townhouse. After three months of dating I asked her to marry me. We were married a year later and just celebrated our eleven year anniversary in 2017. Early on it was hard to know why we clicked and why it worked so well. Now I see that it is because she has taken the time to understand my why. ADHD surfaces in our relationship in many different ways and, together, we have learned to navigate through it all. She knows that much of my behavior stems from my ADHD. Understanding ADHD helped her understand why I behave a certain way in a certain situation. She took the time to understand this and I love her fiercely for that.

Where I can be extremely antisocial, Renee will make up for it by being overly social. She knows that I have about an hour and a half time limit anywhere. She could spend four hours at the pool, while I can barely make it to the hour and a half. She always wants to be on time for social gatherings and is often the last person to leave so sometimes we drive separately, which other people think is odd. If it makes our marriage last, however, I will gladly be labeled odd forever. Renee always wants everyone to like her. I, on the other hand, after a lifetime of people disliking me, have learned that their opinions of me do not define me. She always makes sure that everyone is happy. When I might look like the very face of selfishness, Renee is the very face of selflessness.

She is my number one fan.

She lets me hyperfocus. She will roll her eyes at me but will listen to me talk about whatever it is I'm stuck on for as long as I need to. She tries to talk me down from impulsive decisions and maintains about a 75% success rate. She knows, however, that my number one priority is making sure that we are secure as a family and I would never do anything to jeopardize that. Therefore, while I might be impulsive, every decision I impulsively make is also somehow backed by thought and consideration for what is best for the family.

She is patience personified.

She does everything for the children and the home. She has to ask me at least five times to do a task before I remember to actually do it. When I am explosive, she is calm. When I want to move on, she wants to rehash. When I am distracted, she is on track. When I am meticulous about something, she is flighty. When I have the street smarts, she has the book smarts. Yet, together, we are passionate about the things that matter. We are partners.

Sometimes I try to appease her and sometimes she tries to appease me. It's a balance. We each give and we each take. I know we are blessed. I hope you, your young children, your teenagers, your parents, your future spouses, your friends, and the many strangers out there who are not truly strangers because they are all a part of our ADHD community, will be blessed too. It's as simple and as complex as finding your person and telling them *your* why.

At the end of the story, our hero, Spaz, got the girl.

CONCLUSION:

A CALL TO ACTION

Somewhere along the line we were taught that "normal" is good and being "different" is flawed. Why does the term "different" have a negative connotation? Why, when we are talking about how the ADHD brain is "different", does that have to imply that it is bad/impaired/disabled? What if I told you that it doesn't have to imply that? What if I told you that we don't need to keep that negative connotation? You might ask me, "How is that possible?" Renee and I propose a four-step process: Reflection, Education, Unification, Proclamation.

Step One: Reflection

The first step relies on the ADHDer's ability to look inward. If you are a parent of a child with ADHD, you can do this step with your child. Earlier in the book we talked about rumination and the slippery slope of negative talk in the mind of a person with ADHD. The slope is steep and can spiral out of control, ultimately bringing an ADHDer to their breaking point. To help prevent this, the person with ADHD needs to do some reflection. This can be as simple and as cliché as "count your blessings".

When self-doubt creeps in, I make a list in my mind. I list the accomplishments I have achieved, the hardships I have overcome, and, most importantly, I list the good people in my life. When I count my blessings they include my beautiful children, my loving and understanding wife, our beautiful home, my successful career, and our friends and family. When I think of those things, the naysayers no longer matter.

While reflecting, it is essential to evaluate your relationships. Are you surrounding yourself with the right people? Do they lift you up or do they bring you down? If you have people around you that feed into the negative talk, get rid of them. If the naysayers in your life are the people who love you the most, let them know that you need a positive mindset. They may simply be lacking knowledge about ADHD. It's your responsibility to educate them.

Step Two: Education.

In all of her years as an educator, Renee never received professional development focused on ADHD or other learning disabilities. There were no informational sessions on what special educators do and how they could help you as well as the students you have in common. As ironic as it sounds, education for educators is woefully lacking. If the educators who are left in charge of children with ADHD do not know much about the condition, can we expect the rest of the world to know anything about it?

In the various diversity training seminars that I have had over the course of my career, I have never heard anyone address ADHD. There has been no mention of it as a disability and no instruction on how it could affect someone with it and/or those around the ADHDer in the work place.

The only reason our oldest daughter knows about ADHD is because we have told her all about it. Children do not learn about the disorder in health class. Schools do not have books featuring ADHD characters.

We, as a nation, need to get educated. While it is important that people who are affected by ADHD be educated on the symptoms and causes of the condition, it is also important that the rest of society be educated on it as well. Ignorance is not bliss. Ignorance is dangerous. When people do not understand something, they fear it. However, education on ADHD alone is not enough. ADHD can be listed in the category of invisible illnesses. Invisible illnesses are often misunderstood and misdiagnosed. We need to broaden awareness for these conditions. Similarly, we need to further educate people on the rights and laws associated with these conditions. We learn not to give peanuts to someone who has an anaphylactic allergy, which is considered an invisible condition. But do we make this person feel like they are broken because they can't eat a peanut? Do we degrade them or make fun of them because their body can't process peanut the way a "normal" body can? Do we attempt to force peanuts down their throat thinking that if we just urge them long or hard enough, that they will be able to eat them? No. Of course not. If people are informed and educated about something, an understanding based on that knowledge should arise. The educated will learn that minds can work differently, yet still work equally. They will see that ADHD is not an excuse to behave a certain way, but that it does influence the way people with the disorder behave.

Let's think outside of the box by realizing that there are people who spend their entire lives living outside of the box. As this education grows, so will the need to re-evaluate what it means to have ADHD which brings us to the next phase.

Step Three: Unification.

This is where change can happen. People diagnosed with ADHD need to change their thinking in regard to our "disorder". Renee and I ask ADHDers out there to agree that, while ADHD makes us different than the norm, it *only* makes us different, not flawed. If you Google "Is ADHD a gift?" you will get a plethora of answers ranging from the very affirmative "yes" to the extraordinarily negative "no". These two opposing sides are constantly at war with one another, but if you look up the word "gift" in the Merriam Webster Dictionary, you will find the following definition: "a notable capacity, talent, or endowment" ("Gift"). ADHD, by this definition, could certainly be seen as a gift. It is merely a notable neurological distinction that makes us atypical. It *is* a gift.

When my wife, Renee, holds her workshops for parents of children with ADHD, she tells me that she posts signs leading to it that merely say, "Parent Workshop". Why is she deliberately vague and misleading? Because she acknowledges that there is a stigma associated with ADHD. She often finds parents who don't want to admit that their child even has ADHD, or who will only seek her out in private because they are afraid of "outing" themselves. Although these parents should be commended for wanting to get help, I assert that by hiding from the world they are only hurting their children's hope for a progressive and accepting society.

In writing this section, I Googled "ADHD definition". A popular resource, The Mayo Clinic, was the first site to pop up. Here is their definition:

> Attention-deficit/hyperactivity disorder (ADHD) is a chronic condition that affects millions of children and often continues into adulthood. ADHD includes a combination of persistent problems, such as difficulty sustaining attention, hyperactivity and impulsive behavior.
>
> Children with ADHD also may struggle with low self-esteem, troubled

relationships and poor performance in school. Symptoms sometimes lessen with age. However, some people never completely outgrow their ADHD symptoms. But they can learn strategies to be successful.

While treatment won't cure ADHD, it can help a great deal with symptoms. Treatment typically involves medications and behavioral interventions. Early diagnosis and treatment can make a big difference in outcome.

(Mayo Clinic Staff)

Thousands of newly diagnosed people might Google this same term and be confronted with The Mayo Group's definition. This unfortunate description might be their first introduction to the world of Attention Deficit Hyperactive Disorder. Now imagine a world where this definition included the world "gift", and where it was not implied that having ADHD meant there was something profoundly wrong with you.

We need a unified front of people with a common language: that ADHD, while it is different and has its downsides, also has powerful upsides and advantages. We must insist that it is just a matter of honing in on those strengths and using them to be successful because of them—not in spite of them.

Step Four: Proclamation

As it stands, proclamation is currently the hardest step. If, however, steps one and two are accomplished, proclamation could come easily. Proclamation is our final suggestion for how to break down the negative connotation of our "different" brains. It entails that everyone with ADHD proclaim that they have Attention Deficit Hyper Active Disorder. I am not urging everyone to feel like they must "out" themselves constantly, but I am suggesting that those of us who have it and their loved ones learn to talk about it openly. If we have completed step two properly, then we can talk about ADHD from an educated standpoint with other people who are educated as well.

I, of all people, understand the hesitancy behind admitting to others that you have ADHD. You're afraid of being labeled, mocked, or even discriminated against because of your disability. Unfortunately, I can't assure you that this will not happen. I can assure you, however, that if you stay tight-lipped about it, then you are part of the problem. Think of the successes you may have had in your life thus far. If you're an adult with ADHD, maybe you've found a job that uses your talents and keeps you motivated to keep going day after day. If you're a parent of a child with ADHD, maybe you've figured out how to get your child to school on time every day. If you're a spouse of someone with ADHD, maybe you've learned not to take it personally when your mate remembers that he or she has a meeting, but forgets that it is on your anniversary. Imagine if you could share these successes, no matter how inconsequential they may seem to you, with other people who have ADHD or with people who know that you have ADHD and are able to achieve goals just like any other "normal brained" person. Perhaps you'd give other people ideas, motivation, or hope in a time when they feel that there is none. Success stories are a great resource for people who are hurting. Why not share yours?

We have not come close to achieving proclamation, although there has been a surge of celebrities and people in visible, high-powered positions that have recently come forward and talked about their experiences with ADHD. I find these stories inspirational, which is part of why I chose to write my own story. Writing this, however, only reaffirmed to us that we are nowhere near becoming an accepting society. During this process, some people close to me urged me not to write this book. They feared I would be exploiting myself. They suggested that I could ruin future job opportunities by admitting that I was "mentally ill". These sentiments are exactly why my story, and the stories of others like me, need to be told. Even the stories that seem to be riddled with sadness, oppression, and hopelessness are part of what made me the me that I am today. Who am I?

I am Spaz. I am the face of ADHD. If you are too, or you know someone who is, proclaim it with me.

WORKS CITED

"10 Problems That Could Mean Adult ADHD." *WebMD*. WebMD, n.d. Web. 26 June 2017. <http://www.webmd.com/add-adhd/guide/10-symptoms-adult-adhd#1>

Amen, Daniel G. *Healing ADD: the breakthrough program that allows you to see and heal the six types of attention deficit disorder.* New York: Berkley, 2002. Print.

A Guide to Disability Rights Laws. N.p., n.d. Web. 24 Jan. 2017.

"About - choice, magazine of professional coaching." *Choice, the magazine of professional coaching.* N.p., n.d. Web. 07 Jan. 2017. <www.choice-online.com>

"Attention Deficit Hyperactivity Disorder: Causes of ADHD." *WebMD*. WebMD, n.d. Web. 20 Sept. 2016. < http://www.webmd.com/add-adhd/guide/adhd-causes>

Barkley, Russell A. *Taking charge of ADHD: the complete, authoritative guide for parents.* New York: The Guilford Press, 2013. Print.

"Brain Matures a Few Years Late in ADHD, But Follows Normal Pattern." *National Institute of Mental Health.* U.S. Department of Health and Human Services, 12 Nov. 2007. Web. 31 July 2017.

"Business and Life Coach Training." *Choice, the magazine of professional coaching.* p. 38 Volume 7:Number 3, n.d. Web. 26 July 2017.

Cardone, Grant. *The 10x rule: the only difference between success and failure.* Hoboken, NJ: Wiley, 2011. Print.

CHADD – The National Resource on ADHD. "Professional Directory on ADHD | CHADD." *CHADD – The National Resource on ADHD.* N.p., n.d. Web. 25 Oct. 2016.

Chronis-Tuscano, PhD Andrea. "Very Early Predictors of Adolescent Depression and Suicide Attempts in Children With Attention-Deficit/Hyperactivity Disorder." *Archives of General Psychiatry.* American Medical Association, 04 Oct. 2010. Web. 17 Feb. 2017. <http://jamanetwork.com/journals/jamapsychiatry/fullarticle/210897>

"Cope." *Dictionary.com.* Dictionary.com, n.d. Web. 29 June 2016.

Disability Discrimination. N.p., n.d. Web. 14 Mar. 2017. <https://www.eeoc.gov/laws/types/disability.cfm>

"Divorce Rate in U.S. Drops to Nearly 40-Year Low." *Time*. Time, n.d. Web. 02 Aug. 2017.

"Dr Russell Barkley - ADHD Is Not A Gift." *YouTube*. YouTube, 15 June 2015. Web. 28 July 2017.

Expert, Patient, and Eileen Bailey. "How ADHD Impairs Executive Functioning - Organization at Work - ADHD | HealthCentral." *HealthCentral: Health News and Advice. Trusted Medical Information*. Healthcentral, 11 Apr. 2017. Web. 18 May 2017.

"Free Appropriate Public Education under Section 504." *Home*. US Department of Education (ED), n.d. Web. 23 Apr. 2017.

Friedman, Richard A. "Opinion | A Natural Fix for A.D.H.D." *The New York Times*. The New York Times, 31 Oct. 2014. Web. 2 Nov. 2016. <https://www.nytimes.com/2014/11/02/opinion/sunday/a-natural-fix-for-adhd.html>

"Gift." *Merriam-Webster*. Merriam-Webster, n.d. Web. 18 June 2017. <https://www.merriam-webster.com/dictionary/gift>

Hallowell, Edward. "ADHD Overview." Drhallowell.com. N.p., n.d. Web. 25 Apr. 2017.

Hallowell, Edward M., and John J. Ratey. *Delivered from distraction getting the most out of life with attention deficit disorder.* New York: Ballantine, 2006. Print.

"Home." *Psychology Glossary.* N.p., n.d. Web. 4 Apr. 2017. <https://www.psychology-lexicon.com/cms/glossary/34-glossary-a/5010-attention-deficit-hyperactivity-disorder.html?highlight=WyJhZGhkIl0=>

"Is ADHD an evolutionary gift in a rapidly changing world?" *Activist Post.* N.p., 11 Aug. 2015. Web. 28 July 2017. <http://www.activistpost.com/2012/03/is-adhd-evolutionary-gift-in-rapidly.html>

"Is Your Child Struggling in School? | Kids Life Magazine." *Locable.* N.p., n.d. Web. 30 Aug. 2017.

Mayo Clinic Staff. "Attention-deficit/hyperactivity disorder (ADHD) in children." Mayo Clinic. Mayo Foundation for Medical Education and Research, 11 Mar. 2016. Web. 11 July 2017. < http://www.mayoclinic.org/diseases-conditions/adhd/home/ovc-20196177>

"Reward Deficiency Syndrome (RDS)." *The Gale Encyclopedia of Mental Health.* Encyclopedia.com, n.d. Web. 15 Sept. 2016.

"Ritalin (Methylphenidate Hcl): Side Effects, Interactions, Warning, Dosage & Uses." *RxList*. N.p., n.d. Web. 15 Oct. 2016.

"Ruminate." *Merriam-Webster*. Merriam-Webster, n.d. Web. 26 July 2016. <https://www.merriam-webster.com/dictionary/ruminate>

Staff, Science X. "One-third of women with ADHD report being sexually abused during childhood." *Medical Xpress - medical research advances and health news.* Medical Xpress, 15 Apr. 2015. Web. 6 July 2017.

U.S. Department of Labor - Office of Federal Contract Compliance Programs (OFCCP) - Federal Contractor Selection System (FCSS) - Questions and Answers. N.p., n.d. Web. 26 Jan. 2017. <(https://www.ada.gov/cguide.htm)>

"Wellbutrin (Bupropion Hcl): Side Effects, Interactions, Warning, Dosage & Uses." *RxList*. N.p., n.d. Web. 30 May 2017. <http://www.rxlist.com/wellbutrin-drug.htm>